CW00482167

SLEIGHED TO DEATH

SLEIGHED TO DEATH

by Peter Gordon

JOSEF WEINBERGER PLAYS

LONDON

SLEIGHED TO DEATH
First published in 2017
by Josef Weinberger Ltd
12-14 Mortimer Street, London W1T 3JJ
www.josef-weinberger.com / plays@jwmail.co.uk

ISBN: 978 0 85676 370 0

Printed by Short Run Press Ltd, Exeter

SLEIGHED TO DEATH was first presented under the title DONG DING MURDER ME ON HIGH by Talking Scarlet at The Haymarket, Basingstoke, on January 25th 2017, prior to a national UK tour. The cast was as follows:

SIR WALTON GATES	Jeffrey Holland
MORAG MCKAY	Natasha Grey
GRACE GATES	Anna Brecon
EMMA GATES	Carly Day
JAMES WASHINGTON	Oliver Mellor
SERGEANT PRATT	David Callister
CONSTABLE POTTER	Polly Smith
ARCHIE GATES	Mark Little

Directed by Patric Kearns

Designed by Geoff Gilder

Lighting Design by Keith Tuttle

CAST OF CHARACTERS

SIR WALTON GATES

MORAG McKAY, Sir Walton's secretary

GRACE GATES, Sir Walton's wife

EMMA GATES, Sir Walton's daughter

JAMES WASHINGTON, an adventurer

SERGEANT PRATT

CONSTABLE POTTER, a female police constable

ARCHIE GATES, Sir Walton's brother (naturalised Australian)

The action of the play takes place in the sitting room of a large country house on Christmas Eve in the mid 1930s.

ACT ONE

Scene One: Mid afternoon, Christmas Eve

Scene Two: One hour later, dusk

ACT TWO

Scene One: Five minutes later

Scene Two: Late evening

ACT ONE

Scene One

*The action takes place in the mid 1930s sitting room of
the large country house of* SIR WALTON GATES. *It is mid-
afternoon on Christmas Eve. Left centre are French
windows leading off to a garden path. Stage right is a
fireplace in which a fire is burning, upstage of which is a
door which leads off to a hallway. Next to the door is a light
switch.*

*Stage left, a door leads off to an office. In the corner,
upstage left, is a Christmas tree, decorated with tinsel and
baubles. Under the tree are a number of wrapped presents.
Right of the French windows are a chair and a sideboard,
upon which are a telephone, decanters and glasses. Centre
right is a settee, in front of which is a low occasional table.
Centre left is a small table and chair. Down left is a chair
and low occasional table, upon which is a table lamp.
Down right is a chair. Various documents and files are
haphazardly strewn around the room.*

The room is dimly lit as WALTON *enters from the hallway. He
is aged in his mid-fifties. He comes from a wealthy, upper
class, landed family but is not terribly bright and has an
irritating laugh. He limps quite heavily. As he enters he is
enthusiastically singing 'Hark the Herald Angels Sing'.*

WALTON   (*clearly struggling for the words*) Hark the
              Herald . . . pom pom pom pom, Glory to the . . .
              pom pom pom . . . Peace on earth and pom pom
              pom pom . . . (*Shaking his head, giving up and
              warming himself in front of the fire.*)

              (MORAG MCKAY *enters from the office. She
              is a dour Scotswoman with a strong accent,
              aged around sixty. Although she is* WALTON'S
              secretary he is rather intimidated by her.)

MORAG   (*slightly flustered*) Sir Walton . . . what are you
             doing here?

WALTON   (*taken aback*) I live here, Mrs McKay,
             (*Laughing.*) haw haw.

MORAG   That may be so, but you should be taking
             your afternoon nap. I can generally set my
             clock by the regularity of your habits . . .
             (*Disapproving.*) both the good and the bad!

WALTON   Oh, I don't have any bad habits . . . when you're
             born into the right class of family they're
             merely considered to be eccentricities . . . haw
             haw. Thing is, woke myself up snoring and
             can't get off again. Too much going on up here,
             don't you see. (*Tapping his head.*)

MORAG   (*raising her eyebrows, dismissively*) Aye,
             whatever you say, Sir Walton . . . (*Moving to
             the table lamp and switching it on.*) I'm sure all
             your responsibilities must weigh awful heavy.

WALTON   Ah, well . . . uneasy lies the head, Mrs McKay.
             Thing is, I can't switch off, that's the problem
             . . . big ideas, thick and fast.

MORAG   (*moving to the main light switch and turning it
             on*) Aye, well, in my experience most of your
             ideas are from the thicker end of the spectrum!

WALTON   Oh, don't be such a tease, Mrs McKay!

MORAG   Anyway, if you're needing me I'm afraid it's
             quite out of the question. I'm awful busy trying
             to rectify the mountainous problems created by
             all your previous big ideas!

WALTON   Oh, you carry on, Mrs McKay . . . don't mind
              me . . . quiet as a mouse, haw haw . . . scout's
              honour.

              (MORAG *exits to her office, shutting the door
              behind her.* WALTON *potters around the room,
              singing, not quite sure what to do with himself.*)

              Pom pom pom a Merry Christmas, pom pom
              pom a merry Christmas, pom pom pom a Merry
              Christmas . . . (*Pausing as he picks up a couple
              of sheets of typed paper, peering at them and
              then shaking his head.*) . . . and a pom pom
              New Year. (*Calling out as he moves towards
              the office door.*) Mrs McKay, do you have a
              moment, please?

              (WALTON *reaches the door but almost collides
              with* MORAG, *who surprises him as she comes
              through the door, quickly shutting it behind
              her.*)

              Oh, I say . . . haw haw . . . you almost had me
              toppled over there!

MORAG   (*glaring at him irritably and impatiently*) Aye,
              Sir Walton, what would it be this time? These
              constant interruptions are a terrible irritation.

WALTON   Frightfully sorry but totally unavoidable I'm
              afraid. (*Waving the papers at her.*) These are
              entirely the wrong papers, Mrs McKay . . .
              entirely wrong.

MORAG   (*waving her hand, indicating all the other
              papers*) Then perhaps you might wish to avail
              yourself of some of the others you've left
              littered about the place!

WALTON   (*waving his arms helplessly*) But which ones?
                I was rather hoping to fine-tune my speech for
                the RSPB dinner.

MORAG   Aye, well, I'm surprised they abide you as their
                patron, considering you spend half your days
                blasting their clientele out of the sky. Anyway,
                that's the function you attended last week, Sir
                Walton!

WALTON   (*genuinely surprised*) Me . . . I didn't did I?
                Oh, no, no, surely not. I should know . . . I was
                there!

MORAG   Well that's where I instructed the taxi to take
                you, so I've no doubt that's where you were
                delivered. (*Scolding.*) Do you never check your
                diary?

WALTON   Well, I rather thought that was more your
                department . . . I can't be expected to know
                everything . . . I'm a Knight of the Realm, haw
                haw.

MORAG   Aye, well it's a joint responsibility, so I'd be
                obliged if you'd remember that in the future.
                Now, if my memory serves me correctly,
                your next free meal is courtesy of the British
                Footwear Association.

WALTON   (*blankly*) No! Good Lord, is it really? But I've
                already delivered that speech.

MORAG   To the RSPB? It would hardly seem to be
                appropriate!

WALTON   It would certainly explain the muted reception.
                That joke about their outfit being a load of old
                cobblers fell quite flat. You must send them an
                apology . . . explain that it was all your fault.

MORAG   Mine!

WALTON   Well, I'm afraid that's how society works, Mrs
            McKay. The upper classes make the mistakes,
            the middle classes shoulder the blame and the
            working classes bear the consequences. It's a
            system that's served well for centuries . . . haw
            haw.

MORAG   I despair, Sir Walton! Whatever are we going
            to do with you? Now, if there's nothing else
            concerning you, I'll be getting back to my
            work.

WALTON   Oh, absolutely . . . you carry on. (*Throwing the
            papers down and checking his watch.*) Probably
            about time for a snifter actually . . . don't want
            to go exhausting myself.

MORAG   (*disapproving*) Aye well, you know my thoughts
            on drinking at this hour, Sir Walton.

WALTON   Oh, don't be such a spoilsport, Mrs McKay.
            Father always maintained that the cogs of
            government would grind to a halt if they
            weren't liberally oiled with alcohol. Besides,
            it's Christmas Eve.

MORAG   Aye, but that's no excuse for intemperance
            during the rest of the year. It'll be the death of
            you, Sir Walton . . . the death of you!

WALTON   Ah, well . . . (*Cheerfully.*) guilty as charged.
            (*Confidentially.*) Tell you what, I'll just have
            the one now and you can take all the other
            offences into account when you pronounce
            sentence. Haw haw. (*Pointing to the scattered
            papers.*) Be a good chap and clear all this mess
            away would you?

MORAG   Aye, well, it was you who created the mess in
             the first place.

             (MORAG *moves around the room, collecting
             and sorting papers as* WALTON *moves to the
             sideboard and starts to pour himself a drink.*
             GRACE, *his wife, enters from the hall. She
             is aged around thirty five and is attractive,
             sophisticated, very well-spoken, immaculately
             dressed and wears an expensive pearl necklace,
             and a diamond ring. As she enters, she and*
             MORAG *exchange icy glances.*)

WALTON   Ah, Grace . . . just in time to join me for one?
             I've knocked off for Christmas.

GRACE   Quite right, darling . . . you work far too hard.
             (*Wrinkling her nose in distaste.*) I've just heard
             Emma's car arriving, so a gin is definitely the
             order of the day.

WALTON   And tonic, my dear?

GRACE   I said Emma has arrived . . . so a very long,
             very strong, very straight gin will be absolutely
             perfect. She's become impossibly bohemian
             since she went off to London.

WALTON   (*pouring two drinks*) You really could make a
             bit more of an effort with her . . . I mean, she
             is my only child . . . haw haw. (*Leering and
             winking at* GRACE.) So far anyway.

GRACE   Well, don't get any big ideas on that score,
             darling . . . childbirth and all of the subsequent
             inconvenience is altogether too exhausting a
             prospect to contemplate.

WALTON   We could get a nanny. I never really saw
             Mother until I was about ten. She was

frightfully sporty and for years I thought she was the tennis coach. It was quite a shock to find out we were related. (*Moving to* GRACE *and handing her a drink as he tries to slip an arm around her.*) What do you say?

GRACE   (*shrugging him off and glancing at* MORAG) Please, Walton. Not while the paid help is present.

(WALTON *winces and glances at* MORAG *to see her reaction.*)

MORAG   Personal private secretary if you please, Lady Gates . . . and if I was only interested in the payment, then I can assure you that I could get far more agreeable remuneration elsewhere.

WALTON   Oh, don't take on so, Mrs McKay. It was just a slip of the tongue wasn't it, my dear?

GRACE   (*smiling falsely at* MORAG) Yes, of course it was. I'm sure you're an absolute treasure . . . all of that shorthand and whatever is terribly clever. It must be so fulfilling to have a trade.

(EMMA *bursts into the room from the hallway. She is* WALTON'S *daughter, is in her mid twenties and is gushing, excitable and naive and has great difficulty pronouncing the letter 'r'. She is dressed in 1930s bohemian style. She is followed by* JAMES, *who is in his thirties, handsome, sporty, supremely confident and prone to striking exaggerated manly postures. When* GRACE *sees him, she shows a slight but barely discernible reaction which is missed by all but* JAMES. *Throughout the following action there is a clear but discreet tension between them.*)

EMMA   (*rushing to* WALTON, *excitedly*) Daddy, we're
                here! I've been looking forward to Christmas
                for simply ages and ages!

                (EMMA *and* WALTON *exchange a hug.*)

GRACE   (*sarcastic*) Yes, we've been quite ecstatic with
                excitement ourselves, haven't we, darling?

WALTON   Oh, absolutely! Marvellous to see you, haw
                haw.

EMMA   (*coldly*) Hello, Grace. (GRACE *mouths a very
                insincere kiss towards* EMMA. *Brighter.*) And
                Mrs McKay?

MORAG   Aye, welcome back, Miss Emma. I trust you
                had a good journey?

EMMA   Oh, terrific . . . James drives so quickly. I
                thought my poor little car would just explode
                or something . . . which it didn't . . . luckily!
                (*Turning back to* JAMES.) Daddy, this is James.
                (*Turning back to* WALTON.) He's just returned
                from a trip to Africa . . . isn't that fun!

JAMES   (*moving to* WALTON *and shaking his hand
                enthusiastically and excessively, much
                to* WALTON'S *obvious discomfort*) James
                Washington. Delighted to meet you, sir. I know
                it seems dashed impertinent to foist myself
                upon you like this but when Emmsie found out
                that I was alone for Christmas she insisted that
                I joined in your festivities. I hope you don't
                mind, sir?

EMMA   Of course he doesn't. Daddy?

WALTON   No, not at all. More the merrier, haw haw.

EMMA   James is astonishingly brilliant. He's . . . oh,
              gosh . . . well he's just absolutely amazing
              really . . . (*Thinking hard.*) he's a rock
              climber, a writer, a botanist . . . oh, and an
              anthropologist. Isn't that stupendous? I can't
              even spell half the things he does!

JAMES   I'm a pretty keen photographer as well but I
              wouldn't count myself as a fully fledged expert
              at any of them. Just manage to muddle through
              somehow. Oh, and I simply adore flying.

GRACE   Really? For a man of such diverse talents I
              imagine you don't even require the mechanical
              assistance of an aeroplane for that!

JAMES   (*turning to* GRACE *and smiling*) And you
              obviously must be Lady Gates? Emmsie's told
              me all about you.

GRACE   Yes, I'm sure she has.

              (JAMES *moves to* Grace, *dropping to one knee
              and taking her hand, which she reluctantly
              allows.*)

JAMES   (*kissing her hand and then holding it for just
              a fraction too long before standing*) As it
              happens, the ability to fly unassisted would be
              a godsend. Afraid I don't have the money for
              my own kite.

EMMA   James manages all of his expeditions on an
              absolute shoe-string . . . (*Giggling.*) I simply
              don't know how he does it. The poor man hasn't
              got a bean to his name.

JAMES   (*philosophical*) Oh, luck of the draw I'm afraid
              . . . right family . . . wrong son. Eldest brother
              got the title and estate, middle brother got the

cash and I got father's fly fishing tackle and
mother's wicked sense of mischief! Wouldn't
change it for the world.

WALTON   Splendid. Pity we're out of season. Could have
have taken you out to try for a few salmon.
Bagged some monsters last year, haw haw.

JAMES   I would have enjoyed that, sir. Once had to
survive on raw fish for several months when
I was escaping from some native types in the
Amazon.

EMMA   Yuk! Raw fish? How horrid . . . I'd be sick.

JAMES   Couldn't risk a campfire . . . amazing sense
of smell those chaps had. Marvellous people.
Thought I was cutting along with them pretty
well until they started eyeing up my head. It
came down to a pretty stark choice . . . have it
chopped off and shrunk or tootle off and make
myself scarce!

GRACE   You'll need to be very wary around here then
. . . (*Laughing.*) Mrs McKay can be terribly
fearsome. She could shrivel your head with a
glance!

WALTON   Mrs McKay? Oh, yes, quite so . . . haw haw . . .
frightfully good.

MORAG   (*coldly*) I think you'll find that the McKay's
have an enviable reputation for their
lighthearted cordiality, Lady Gates, so I
would be grateful if you'd direct your hilarity
elsewhere, if you'd be so kind?

GRACE   Cordiality perhaps but clearly little sense of
humour, I think. That will be all for now . . .

I'm sure you must have lots of vital filing or
paper clipping to complete.

MORAG   Sir Walton?

WALTON   Yes . . . that's fine, thank you.

MORAG   (*moving towards the office door*) And I'd
            appreciate no further disturbances. You may be
            finished for the festive season but some of us
            still need to attend to your vital interests.

WALTON   Oh, absolutely. Don't take offence, Mrs McKay
            . . . it was just a spot of . . .

            (WALTON *is cut-off as* MORAG *exits to the office,
            pointedly shutting the door.*)

            Ah . . . well.

GRACE   Ghastly woman. No mistaking Mrs McKay for
            a ray of sunshine!

EMMA   Oh, don't be so beastly to her, Grace. I don't
            know how Daddy would manage without her!

GRACE   Yes, but then he has been somewhat devoid of
            any sensible help from within the family for
            many years! Now, James, please, please, tell
            me you don't claim musicianship amongst your
            many talents. Emma's guest last Christmas
            insisted on boring us with his violin! My
            husband overheard from an adjoining room and
            imagined we'd acquired a vocal, stray cat.

WALTON   That's true, so I did, haw haw. Frightful noise
            . . . peculiar chap.

EMMA   (*sharply, to* JAMES) Except Daddy wasn't her
            husband then. Poor Mummy hadn't been dead
            for very long.

WALTON   (*hurriedly*) Quite so, but let's not dwell on the
            past, eh? Very important to move on . . . best
            foot forward, chin up . . . stiff upper lip.

EMMA   But Daddy, it was horrid . . . our first
            Christmas without her! (*To* JAMES.) Then, soon
            after that, we had an intruder who broke who
            in and beat daddy nearly half to death with his
            own cricket bat!

WALTON   Dashed unsporting!

GRACE   And rather an exaggeration, Emma, darling!
            A broken leg may not be much fun but it's
            hardly life threatening. I'm sure our adventurer,
            James, would have hopped along on his
            expeditions regardless!

WALTON   (*flexing his bad leg thoughtfully*) Worst cricket
            injury I've ever had. (*Tapping his head.*) Taken
            a few blows to the old pate over the years but
            it's never seemed to do me much harm . . . not
            that anyone could tell anyway, haw haw.

JAMES   I open the batting and bowling for the County,
            when I can fit it around my schedule. (*Miming
            the execution of a perfect cover drive.*) Nothing
            to beat the sound of leather on willow is there,
            sir!

WALTON   Absolutely not . . . haw haw . . . now that is
            music to the old ears. You two chaps care for a
            drink?

EMMA   Usual for me please, Daddy and the same for
            James. (*To* JAMES.) Now, as our guest you must

help yourself whenever you care for one . . .
(*Giggling.*) just so long as you don't get too
squiffy!

WALTON   (*moving to pour two gin and tonics*) Yes,
absolutely . . . except for my vintage malts
of course . . . haw, haw . . . need special
dispensation to touch those.

EMMA   Now, we simply must find something silly for
you to wear, James. Mummy was such fun. She
absolutely insisted that, at Christmas, everyone
must wear fancy dress. Oh, the times we had.
We used to roar with laughter!

GRACE   I really don't think I much care to continue
with that nonsense, Emma, darling . . . it's all
far too tedious for words.

EMMA   But we must! Daddy? (*There is an
uncomfortable silence.*) Daddy, tell her!

WALTON   (*to* GRACE) Well, I don't suppose it would do
any harm would it, my dear? A spot of seasonal
joviality.

GRACE   (*cold*) Fine, darling, as you wish . . . far be
it from me to interfere in the running of my
own household. Lord knows what that brother
of yours will wear . . . he's quite ridiculous
enough as it is.

EMMA   (*in surprise*) Daddy's brother?

WALTON   (*to* GRACE) Oh, I say, that was meant to be a bit
of a surprise.

EMMA   (*with growing excitement*) He's not here? Uncle
Archie . . . actually here?

WALTON   Turned up yesterday . . . completely out of the
              blue!

EMMA   (*shrieking with delight*) All the way from
              Australia? How amazingly brilliant! What's he
              like?

GRACE   Antipodean bumpkin would sum him up more
              than adequately. He seems to have heartily
              embraced the Australian culture . . . if one
              could ever call it that!

EMMA   (*to* JAMES) I've been absolutely dying to meet
              him for years. Mummy and Daddy were going
              to visit him last year (*Breaking off.*) . . . but
              then Mummy . . .

GRACE   (*to* WALTON) I really fail to comprehend what
              you and Elizabeth were thinking of, darling.
              (*To* JAMES.) As far as I can gather, James, he's a
              parasitic, ne'er-do-well. He's been scrounging
              off my husband for the last thirty years.

WALTON   Well, not exactly off me, my dear. The chap's
              been perfectly entitled. Father set up a trust
              fund to provide him with a regular income . . .

GRACE   Despite the fact that he'd packed him off to
              Australia in disgrace! The foibles of your
              family never cease to amaze me, darling . . .
              it's a wonder you ever accumulated any wealth
              at all!

WALTON   Ah, but in a family of breeding it's almost
              compulsory to have a wrong 'un kicking about
              . . . haw haw. Anyway, none of us are getting
              any younger and Elizabeth was adamant that I
              go over there and patch things up.

EMMA   (*to* JAMES) After Mummy died, I was
            determined to take her place and travel to
            Australia with Daddy. What a stupendous
            adventure that would have been. Then Daddy's
            broken leg put paid to all our plans.

JAMES   Ah, you'd have adored it, Emmsie. There's
            nothing quite like the sight of Ayres Rock from
            the back of a camel at dawn.

GRACE   But now he's beaten you all to it and landed on
            our doorstep out of the blue, like a very bad
            penny. Oh what joy!

WALTON   Quite so and we mustn't be churlish about it.
            We'll just have to buckle down and make the
            most of it. Have a fine old family Christmas
            together.

GRACE   How sublime. I can hardly wait!

EMMA   So where is he?

WALTON   Said he was taking himself off for a
            'walkabout', whatever that means. I expect he'll
            be back shortly. All of which jolly well reminds
            me. (*Moving towards the office door and
            calling.*) Mrs McKay . . . do you have a moment
            please?

            (*As* WALTON *reaches the door,* MORAG *enters
            from the office, shutting the door behind her.*)

MORAG   (*wearily*) Aye, Sir Walton, I imagine that this
            would be another one of your emergencies?

WALTON   Absolutely. I tasked you with digging out those
            old photographs of Archie and myself. Any
            progress?

MORAG   Aye, well, I've scoured the office from top to
           bottom and they're nowhere to be seen   . . .
           nowhere at all. Perhaps you've stored them
           in the old nursery room, along with the other
           family junk.

WALTON   (*indignant*) That's not junk, Mrs McKay . . .
           it's generations worth of family history . . .
           stretching right back to when we actually had
           to work for a living, haw, haw! You'd best come
           along and assist in the search.

MORAG   Aye, but . . .

WALTON   No buts, Mrs McKay . . . this is absolutely top
           priority.

EMMA   (*gulping the last of her drink*) And me, Daddy
           . . . I'll help. You must come too, James. It's
           an Aladdin's cave up there . . . full of the most
           amazing treasure!

           (WALTON, MORAG *and* EMMA *move to exit to the
           hall.*)

JAMES   Love to, Emmsie, love to, but to tell you the
           truth, I'm absolutely whacked after yesterday's
           rugger match. We had two chaps sent off and I
           had to cover both wings and hooker. Mind if I
           stay down here and relax with my drink?

           (EMMA *looks hesitant about leaving him with*
           GRACE.)

GRACE   Don't worry, Emma, darling. I'll look after
           him.

EMMA   But . . .

GRACE   I promise I won't eat him!

(EMMA *reluctantly exits with* WALTON *and*
MORAG. GRACE *immediately rushes to the door,
checks to make sure that they've gone and then
shuts the door before spinning back, angrily to*
JAMES.)

Kill him, maybe . . . slap him, almost certainly!

JAMES Kiss him, perhaps?

GRACE What the hell are you doing here, James? Two
bad pennies in the space of two days is simply
beyond belief!

JAMES (*standing and smiling disarmingly*) Oh Gracie,
come on. Is that any way to greet an old friend?

GRACE Three years, James. It's been three years since
you walked out.

JAMES Please . . . let's not go through all of that again.
We agreed . . . it was impossible. All you ever
wanted was money and a life of comfort . . . I
couldn't give you that.

GRACE Couldn't or wouldn't? Too busy dashing off
performing manly deeds of derring-do!

JAMES Oh, don't let's argue, Gracie. Your dream's
come true . . . don't begrudge me following
mine.

GRACE My dream? (*Shaking her head.*) . . . You think
that I enjoy this? James, I hate it . . . I detest
it. Married to that man . . . you think that's a
dream?

JAMES But you chose . . .

GRACE   (*snapping*) . . . yes, I chose! Bad choice as it
             turns out but then that's not your problem is it?
             Oh no, nothing was ever your problem.

JAMES   Oh, Gracie, don't be angry with me . . . I can't
             bear it.

GRACE   (*softening*) Oh, James, I'm not angry with
             you . . . not really. Yes, I absolutely despised
             you when you walked out of my life but that
             was my big mistake. That's why I plotted
             and schemed my way into Walton's life. My
             success would somehow be your failure. Oh,
             Walton's a good man . . . a kind man . . . but
             I'm afraid I'm beginning to loathe him . . . his
             ridiculous manner . . . his awful laugh! So,
             James, welcome to my world . . . heaven on the
             outside . . . but on the inside I think my soul is
             descending into hell. I know I'm turning into
             some kind of monster but I'm powerless to stop
             it. And now you turn up here with Emma. Is
             that some kind of a sick joke? We detest each
             other.

JAMES   Oh, she's not so bad. She means well but she's
             not my type at all. I met her at a friend's party
             . . . and then I realised who she was. Maybe
             I was wrong but when she invited me here I
             couldn't resist the chance to see you again.
             Look, if you want me to leave . . .

GRACE   (*sighing*) No, James, that's the last thing I want.
             To tell you the truth, when you walked into the
             room my poor little heart started pounding like
             anything. I just don't see what good can come
             out of you being here.

JAMES   Opening old wounds? (*Tenderly.*) Oh, Gracie,
             you don't have the monopoly on bad choices.
             You'll never know how much I've missed you.

(JAMES *and* GRACE *suddenly fall into each others arms, kissing passionately. Unseen by them,* PRATT *appears, wandering past outside the French window. He is a middle aged, inept, clumsy, walking disaster area. He wears an overcoat and a Santa's hat and beard. He is carrying a collection tin. As he passes the window, he stops and looks inside. Startled to see* JAMES *and* GRACE *kissing, he peers at them open-mouthed for a few seconds before continuing on his way.* JAMES *and* GRACE *separate.*)

JAMES   Did you really mean what you said . . . about Sir Walton?

GRACE   James . . . if I could afford to walk out tomorrow, I would!

JAMES   (*slowly and thoughtfully*) So, what if there was a way . . . a way out of all the dreadful mess I've made of things? Where we could both lead the lives that we want . . . but together . . . forever.

GRACE   James, stop it . . . that's impossible!

JAMES   I've spent my whole life attempting the impossible . . . why stop now? I just need to get my hands on your husband's money. (*Urgently.*) We need to talk . . . somewhere where we won't be disturbed for a while.

GRACE   I could show you to your room. And I'll make it as far away from Emma's as is possible.

JAMES   You don't need to worry about that, I've been the perfect gentleman, as always.

GRACE   (*teasing*) Well that's not how I remember you.

JAMES   Gracie, there's only ever been one girl for me.
             Come on, let's hurry, before the others come
             back.

             (JAMES *and* GRACE *exit to the hallway just
             before* PRATT *reappears outside the French
             windows. He peers through, looking rather
             confused, before tentatively trying the door
             handle. Finding the door unlocked he steps
             into the room, glancing around hopefully and
             shaking the collection tin, which clearly only
             has a single coin inside.*)

PRATT   Hello . . . knock knock . . . is there anybody
             there? (*Receiving no response, he starts singing
             the first lines of a carol.*) Dong ding murder me
             on high . . . in Devon the bells are swinging . . .

             (*He shakes his tin hopefully before becoming
             bored and moving to examine the Christmas
             tree. He accidentally pulls off one of the
             baubles and is trying to reattach it as* EMMA
             enters from the hall. PRATT *immediately hides
             the bauble behind his back, guilty but trying to
             look casual.*)

EMMA   (*as she enters*) James, I was just . . . (*Seeing*
             PRATT *she halts in surprise before shrieking in
             delight.*) Gosh . . . Uncle Archie!

             (PRATT *looks behind himself in surprise,
             thinking that someone else must be there.*)

EMMA   (*suddenly unsure of herself*) It is you isn't it?

PRATT   (*confused*) I believe so, madam. I've always
             been me . . . ever since I was a small boy.

EMMA   And you're Santa . . . what fun!

PRATT   (*modestly*) Ah, don't be fooled by my clever
               disguise . . . I'm not the real Santa Claus.

EMMA   Yes, I realise that.

PRATT   And I haven't brought you a present if that's
               what you were hoping.

EMMA   (*joking*) Oh, how beastly of you . . . too fat for
               the chimney?

PRATT   (*defensively*) Don't be deceived, madam . . .
               lurking beneath this bulbous coat is the body of
               a finely horned athlete.

EMMA   No . . . I meant the present's too fat for . . . !

PRATT   But I haven't brought you one.

EMMA   (*confused, slowly*) No . . . I don't want to be a
               bore but do you think we should start again?

PRATT   From where?

EMMA   The beginning perhaps?

PRATT   A very good idea, madam, you seem somewhat
               un-cohesive. Allow me to reiterate my entrance.
               (*Picking up his collection tin, moving to the
               French windows and tapping on them.*) Knock
               knock . . . Yo ho ho . . . (*Singing.*) dong ding
               merrily . . .

EMMA   Yes?

PRATT   (*shaking the tin before placing it down*) I am
               Sergeant Pratt and I'm soliciting for the Retired
               Police Officers Malevolent Fund.

EMMA   Oh . . . gosh . . . I understand now. (*Giggling*.)
            How silly!

PRATT   (*indignant*) No they're not silly . . . they've
            dedicated many years to public servitude!

EMMA   No . . . (*Pointing to herself.*) me . . . I'm silly. I
            thought that you were someone else.

PRATT   Ah, yes, Santa Claus. It's a very lifelike
            costume isn't it? (*Pulling the false beard off,
            wincing with pain.*) . . . arghh . . . it's fooled
            everybody. I was going to dress as Good King
            Wendy's ass but I'm afraid I'm two legs short of
            a full donkey.

EMMA   Look, I don't have any money immediately to
            hand but . . .

PRATT   No, madam, the act of begging would be
            criminally offensive. What I am offering is a
            performance of my touring peri-pathetic magic
            show.

EMMA   Magic? Wow, how incredible! I do so love
            magic.

PRATT   Really, then you've come to exactly the right
            man. I am a master of delusion. Observe . . .
            this is a small burble from your tree.

            (PRATT *theatrically displays the bauble in his
            hand before removing a handkerchief from his
            pocket and wrapping the bauble in it.*)

            Now, I shall place the burble in my
            handkerchief thusly and then . . . (*Noticing the
            ashtray on the table and picking it up.*) . . . ah,
            this'll do . . . allow me to . . .

(PRATT *places the wrapped bauble on the table and smashes it several times with the ashtray before lifting it back up from the table and theatrically waving his hand over it.*)

Abraca-zebra.

(PRATT *smiles in anticipation as he unfolds the handkerchief but is embarrassed as the shattered pieces of the bauble fall to the floor.*)

Ah . . . (*Casually, as he screws up his handkerchief and places it back in his pocket.*) . . . a bit of glue, it'll be fine. (*Hurriedly.*) May I introduce my assistant?

EMMA   Yes, of course, tremendous.

PRATT   (*moving to the French windows and calling outside*) Porter . . . get yourself in here, at the double . . . come along . . . quickly.

(CONSTABLE MARY POTTER *appears outside the French windows. She is in her mid-twenties and is intelligent and feisty but rather gawky and lacking in self confidence. She is dressed very amateurishly as a fairy, which she is clearly very embarrassed about.*)

POTTER   (*exasperated*) It's Potter, Sarge . . . not Porter.

PRATT   Never mind that . . . hurry up, we haven't got all day.

POTTER   (*to EMMA*) Hello . . . he's hopeless, honest! (*Pointing at her dress, self consciously.*) Sorry . . . it was his idea. (*To PRATT.*) I don't know why I've got to go around looking like this, Sarge . . . this is supposed to be my day off.

PRATT   (*to* EMMA) For the purpose of my theatrical
            delusions I normally employ an intelligent
            and attractive lady assistant. Unfortunately,
            Constable Porter is inedible on both counts but
            I'm afraid she's the best I could find at short
            notice. She is dressed, as you will see, as the
            arch-angel Gabriel.

EMMA   Oh, super, that's brilliant . . . for a moment I
            thought she was a fairy.

POTTER   See, I told you, Sarge! It's not fair making me
            dress up like this. (*To* EMMA.) I look really
            smart in my proper uniform, honest.

PRATT   I'll decide what's fair, Porter. (*To* EMMA.)
            Where would you like me to perform?

EMMA   Oh, gosh. Look . . . I wouldn't want to take
            advantage of you but would it be a frightful
            bore if I asked you to perform for everyone
            later this evening? It would be the most
            amazing fun.

PRATT   Everyone? Oh . . . (*Excitedly.*) you mean I
            would have a large conflagration of people?

EMMA   You'll need to make the arrangements with Sir
            Walton. I'll send him through shall I?

PRATT   Through what? Ah yes, very good. Oh, and I
            wonder if I might borrow your telephone . . .
            by borrow, I don't mean I want to take it away
            with me . . . I just want to talk to it.

EMMA   As you wish, Sergeant.

PRATT   And in the circumstantials please feel free to
            address me by my theatrical numb de plum . . .
            'The Incredible Puzzled Pratt'.

EMMA   (*excitedly and theatrically, pronouncing Pwatt*)
            Wow, 'The Incredible Puzzled Pratt'!

PRATT   No . . . no, Pratt!

EMMA   That's what I said . . . Pratt. Brilliant . . . how
            stupendous!

            (EMMA *skips off to the hall, excitedly.*)

POTTER   Oh, Sarge, do we have to stay until later? It's
            Christmas Eve. I was going to have a bath and
            wash my hair tonight.

PRATT   And that is exactly why I'm against women
            being recruited into the police force. It's no use
            thinking you can just join up and then spend
            all your time at home abluting! You should be
            pleased to be out and about rather than stuck at
            the station making cups of tea.

POTTER   Well, I shouldn't have to make the tea all the
            time. I'd be really good at solving things.

PRATT   Lady policemen solving things? Whatever will
            you want next? It all started going wrong when
            you were given universal suffering to vote!
            (*Moving to the phone and dialling.*) Anyway,
            you're staying here to help, Patter . . . that's a
            direct order from your superfluous officer. I'm
            discom-boobled by it as well . . . I'd planned a
            romantic evening at home with Mrs Pratt.

POTTER   Bet she'll be devastated to miss that, Sarge!

PRATT   (*into the phone*) Ah, hello my love, it's George
            . . . George . . . your husband, George . . . Yes,
            well, I'm afraid there's been a change of plan,
            my love, work I'm afraid . . . What? You're
            wearing what? . . . (*Embarrassed, tugging*

to loosen his collar.) Your best flannelette
nightie? . . . Well, I'm sure you must look very
erratic my love but I'm afraid something's
just popped up (*Hurriedly.*) cropped up . . .
(*Recoiling from the phone.*) . . . Well, there's no
need for that aptitude . . . (*Wincing.*) . . . Yes,
my love, I will be lucky I know but . . . hello?
. . . hello? . . . (*Glancing at* POTTER, *trying
to impress.*) And just you make sure you get
those Brussel sprouts on overnight, woman
. . . (*Wincing.*) Sorry, my love, I thought you'd
gone! . . . Hello? . . . Hello? . . . Ah. (*Putting
the phone back and smiling ruefully at* POTTER.)

POTTER   Sounds like you'll be on the settee tonight,
               Sarge.

PRATT   Oh, no, Mrs Pratt's a very understanding
               woman . . . it's just that she's giving the little
               Pratts an early night and she had plans for me
               to stuff her turkey.

               (ARCHIE GATES *enters through the French
               windows. He is aged around 50 and is a no-
               nonsense, garrulous Australian with a strong
               Australian accent. He wears green trousers
               which have a large hole in the seat. This
               becomes obvious to the audience as he turns to
               close the French windows behind him.*)

ARCHIE   (*as he enters*) G'day. How're you going?

PRATT   (*mystified by the accent*) I beg your pardon?

ARCHIE   I said, G'day.

PRATT   Ah . . . and goody to you too, sir.

ARCHIE   (*looking at* PRATT'S *hat*) I didn't expect to find
              Santa here so soon. Chrissie won't be here for a
              few hours yet, mate.

PRATT   Chrissie? I wasn't even aware she lived here,
              sir.

POTTER   Think he means Christmas, Sarge.

              (ARCHIE *moves towards* POTTER *and* PRATT
              notices the hole in his trousers.)

ARCHIE   (*leering*) And you must be Santa's little helper,
              eh? Well you can help me out any time you like,
              if you get my meaning?

POTTER   (*with obvious distaste*) Yes, I think I do.

ARCHIE   You can drop by and give me my prezzie later
              tonight if you like . . . I've been good as gold
              all year . . . more or less.

PRATT   Excuse me.

ARCHIE   Why, what've you done, mate?

PRATT   (*pointing at his trousers, embarrassed*) It's . . .
              your trousers.

ARCHIE   (*posing*) What about 'em, eh?

PRATT   No . . . no, round the back.

ARCHIE   (*feeling behind*) Oh, crikey . . . my best pair of
              daks! Ah, well, no worries. (*Laughing.*) Hey,
              back in Oz we call that the big 'outback' eh?

              (ARCHIE *starts displaying the hole
              ostentatiously to them both*. PRATT *stares at him
              blankly and* POTTER *looks on distastefully*.)

Get that, mate? Big 'outback', yeah? Get it?

(PRATT *continues to stare blankly.*)

Ah well, please yourself, mate. Anyway, forgive me for being blunt but who the hell are you anyway? Walt didn't mention he had a shed load of people coming over. (*Taking his hand straight from his rear and offering it to* PRATT.) Archie Gates.

PRATT   (*looking at the offered hand dubiously before reluctantly shaking it)* Pratt.

ARCHIE   Well there's no need to be like that, mate, I was just trying to be civil.

PRATT   No, that's me . . . Sergeant Pratt. This is Constable Putter.

POTTER   Potter. (*Coldly, clearly disliking* ARCHIE.) And we're already being attended to by a very nice lady, thank you, sir.

ARCHIE   Ah, I reckon that'd be Lady Gates. Bit of a stunner . . . can't understand why she'd marry a senile old duffer like my brother.

         (WALTON *enters from the hall, closely followed by* MORAG.)

         Ah, speak of the devil.

WALTON   (*moving to* PRATT) Ah Archie, there you are. And you must be this Puzzled Pratt fellow?

ARCHIE   Yeah, well, he's certainly a puzzle to me, Walt, that's for sure . . . fair dinkum, no worries!

WALTON   Thank you, Archie. I'm Sir Walton, I understand you're in the market to do a bit of a turn for us?

PRATT   Not in the market, sir . . . I'm happy to perform right here in the comfort of your own home. Police Officers Malevolent Fund.

POTTER   He means benevolent, sir.

            (PRATT *scowls at her.*)

WALTON   Quite so. It all sounds frightfully philanthropic.

PRATT   No, we're not collecting stamps, sir . . . it's just a few magical tricks.

WALTON   Yes, so I gathered. Chopping people in half . . . that type of thing is it? Haw haw.

PRATT   I perform a wide range of conjugal skills, sir. Unfortunately, I had to poleaxe the sawing in half routine from my act after a rather tragic accident with (*Crossing himself.*) Mrs Pratt's sister.

WALTON   Good Lord. You didn't kill her?

PRATT   Fortunately my lightning reflexology averted fatality, though her left leg was in jeopardy for some weeks.

ARCHIE   Strewth! They managed to save it then?

PRATT   Happily, sir, yes. It's pickled in a jar at the teaching hospital.

            (*They stand open-mouthed before* MORAG *breaks the silence.*)

MORAG   If I might make a remark, Sir Walton?

WALTON   Oh, absolutely, Mrs McKay . . . fire away.

MORAG   It's just that on the evidence so far presented
           . . . I'm not sure that I would wish to engage this
           fellow.

POTTER   (*to* WALTON) It is for a good cause, sir.
           (*Hopefully.*) But if you don't want us we could
           get off home.

ARCHIE   If you ask me, Walt, (*Tapping his head.*)
           the bloke's got a kangaroo loose in the top
           paddock. I'm not sure he's that safe to have
           around.

PRATT   I can assure you, sir, that I'm as safe as
           a hearse. My last application to join the
           Magical Circle was only narrowly rejected by
           unanimous decision.

WALTON   Really? How extraordinary.

PRATT   Although if you prefer, I could offer you
           my one-man nativity show. I start with the
           Immaculate Contraption and go right through
           to the visitation of the three blind men with the
           gold, Frankenstein and manure.

POTTER   Myrrh, Sarge!

WALTON   Oh, no, I'd far prefer the magic show I think.
           How does two guineas sound?

PRATT   I would prefer English currency, sir.

WALTON   Haw, haw . . . very good. How about two
           pounds then?

PRATT   Two pounds, oh, most generous! When would
               you like me to start?

WALTON   Ah, now, there's a question. About an hour I
               expect. It would give us all a chance to freshen
               up first.

PRATT   Very good, sir. There is just one ad-minstrel
               matter to take care of before I begin.

WALTON   Oh, absolutely. Mrs McKay's in command of
               all that sort of business from my end. I'm sure
               she'll assist you.

MORAG   Aye, if that's what you'd like, Sir Walton.
               But be warned . . . in my opinion the man's a
               charlatan . . . nothing but a charlatan.

WALTON   Oh, chin up, Mrs McKay . . . what's the worst
               that can happen? You can watch his show
               as well. It'll be a treat for you. (*Moving and
               exiting through the hall door.*) Come along,
               Archie, let's get out from under the fellow's
               feet. We'll go through to the conservatory and
               I'll introduce you to Emma.

ARCHIE   (*as he exits to the hall*) Yeah, no worries, Walt,
               I'm right behind you. I'll need to change these
               strides though . . . I snagged them on your back
               fence.

               (WALTON *and* ARCHIE *exit.*)

MORAG   I hope you'll not be keeping me for long,
               Sergeant? I have a very heavy schedule.

PRATT   Really? Well, Putter can help you move that
               later . . . after she's brought all my equipment
               in from the car.

POTTER   All of it, Sarge . . . by myself? What about you?

PRATT   Me? I shall take a short stroll in the fresh
              air to compost myself in readiness for the
              performance. It may look as easy as falling
              off a roof to you but it requires great mental
              annuity.

POTTER   (*exiting through the French windows with a
              sigh*) Yes, Sarge . . . whatever you say.

PRATT   (*taking a folded piece of paper and a pencil
              from his pocket*) As for you, Mrs Manky . . . I'd
              like you to pass this highly secretive note to the
              lady of the house.

MORAG   That would be Lady Gates.

PRATT   Oh, Lady Gates . . . yes.

              (PRATT *scrawls a name on the paper, and gives
              it to* MORAG.)

MORAG   Aye, and might I ask what it's about?

PRATT   Certainly not. I'm afraid I can't divulge the
              exact nature of the secretion. (*Tapping his
              nose.*) Suffice to say that I shall be randily
              selecting her to help me with my climatic
              finale. By debriefing her first I can maintain an
              egmatic air. May I rely on your discretion.

MORAG   Aye, I expect so. Will that be all?

PRATT   (*inadvertently in a Scottish accent*) Aye.

MORAG   (*giving* PRATT *a withering look before exiting to
              the hall*) Then I'll pass it to her when I next see
              her.

PRATT   (*to himself in a Scottish accent*) Aye.

                 (PRATT *produces his handkerchief from his
                 pocket and is about to blow his nose when he
                 realises that there are bits of the shattered
                 bauble still in it. He looks around for
                 somewhere to dispose of it, finally tossing it
                 behind the Christmas tree before turning and
                 exiting through the French windows.*)

                 (*Lights fade.*)

Scene Two

*An hour later. The curtains are drawn across the French
windows. On the small table, centre left, are three
headscarves, one red, one green and one white. Hidden
beneath the green scarf are two decks of cards, one red
backed and the other green backed. Hidden beneath the red
scarf is a gun.* ARCHIE *is sitting reading a book as* EMMA
*enters from the hall. She is wearing a sheet over her head,
which completely conceals her except for eye holes.*

EMMA   (*as she enters, speaking in a ghostly voice*)
                 Whoooo . . . whooooo . . . (*In an imitation of*
                 MORAG'S *Scottish accent.*) Och, I am the ghost
                 of Christmas Future . . . whoooo . . . whoooo.

ARCHIE   (*looking up from his book*) In that case, Emma,
                 I shouldn't be here because I won't be coming
                 over at this time of year again! I prefer to eat
                 my Chrissie dinner in the sunshine!

EMMA   (*disappointed at being recognised*) Oh, gosh!
                 How did you know it was me? You were
                 supposed to think it was Mrs McKay!

ARCHIE   Sorry but it hardly takes a genius. At her age,
                Mrs McKay is probably more of a Christmas
                Past kinda Sheila. She's certainly well past her
                best, that's for sure . . . got a face like a half
                sucked lemon.

EMMA   (*removing the sheet*) It's dreadfully hot under
                there! Perhaps you could wear it and I'll come
                as a Christmas pudding or something . . .
                (*Giggling.*) then I could steep myself in lots of
                stupendous brandy.

ARCHIE   Sorry but I've never been a dressing up kinda
                bloke. Afraid you'll just have to put up with me
                in my civvies.

EMMA   Oh, no that won't do at all. But it's just so
                brilliant that you're here in the first place . . .
                after all these years.

ARCHIE   Oh, I've had a mind to get myself over here to
                Blighty for a long time but when I heard you
                and your father were set on visiting Oz, I'd put
                all my pommie plans on the back burner.

EMMA   I was absolutely devastated when we couldn't
                travel. It was rotten luck when Daddy got
                beaten up like that.

ARCHIE   Sounds like it was a nasty incident.

EMMA   Well, the police think it must have been some
                horrid burglar who got disturbed as he snuck
                into Daddy's room to grab some loot. Poor
                Daddy must have muttered something in his
                sleep . . . all he remembers is waking up when
                they whacked his leg with the bat!

ARCHIE   Strewth! And they never caught the mongrel
                who did it?

EMMA   Daddy just glimpsed a shadow moving out of
            the door.

ARCHIE   But what about Grace . . . didn't she catch sight
            of anything?

EMMA   Grace? She's hopeless! Anyway, they weren't
            actually married then . . . they were in separate
            rooms.

ARCHIE   (*leering*) That's what they told you anyway!

EMMA   Uncle Archie! Anyway she and Daddy still have
            separate rooms even now.

ARCHIE   Strewth! The old duffer's even slower than I
            thought! But you obviously don't think too
            much of the new love of your father's life then?

EMMA   Love? Love's got absolutely nothing to do with
            it? I know it's a horrid thing to say but Daddy's
            quite weak really. He couldn't cope when
            Mummy died and she saw her opportunity to
            pounce. I don't know what Daddy sees in her . . .
            he says she's from 'good stock'.

ARCHIE   Makes her sound a bit like a horse!

EMMA   She may have all the airs and graces, but she
            certainly hasn't got any money. That's the only
            reason the beastly woman married Daddy!
            And now he says he may have to reduce my
            allowance because of all her spending! I'd jolly
            well like to smash her with a bat . . . I used to
            be pretty handy with a hockey stick.

ARCHIE   Well as it happens I'm not exactly a big fan of
            Grace either. She's trying to get your father
            to cut off my money completely . . . can you
            believe that?

EMMA   I'd believe anything of her. But she can't do
            it can she . . . I thought it was a trust fund or
            something?

ARCHIE   Nothing a half decent lawyer couldn't drive a
            horse and dunny cart through. If she gets her
            way, I end up with nothing . . . what do you
            make of that?

EMMA   But couldn't you survive without it? I thought
            you had a huge farm?

ARCHIE   Poor grazing land though. Last year we
            produced about enough wool to knit a pair of
            gloves for a one armed man. I'd be ruined.

EMMA   Gosh! (*Thoughtfully.*) Uncle Archie . . . may I
            ask you something?

ARCHIE   Fire away.

EMMA   It's just that . . . nobody would ever tell me.
            Why did grandpapa send you off to Australia
            all those years ago? It wasn't for anything
            really horrid was it . . . you know, like violence
            or something?

ARCHIE   I think that's best left in the past, don't you . . .
            that was between me and your grandfather.

EMMA   (*conspiratorially*) It's just that when I think
            of how Grace is spending all my inheritance,
            I feel so angry and I get these really horrid
            thoughts about how I might get rid of her!
            Thought you might have some ideas.

ARCHIE   Now, girl, you want to be careful who you go
            around saying things like that to . . . you might
            get yourself into a heap of bother!

(GRACE *and* JAMES *enter from the hall.* GRACE *is no longer wearing her necklace.*)

GRACE Ah, what luck . . . Emma and Archie . . . (*Sarcastically.*) the focal point of scintillating conversation, no doubt. But then, you haven't met Archie yet, have you?

JAMES (*moving to* ARCHIE *and shaking his hand*) No, I haven't but I've been looking forward to it enormously. James Washington.

ARCHIE Good to meet you, mate. Archie Gates.

EMMA (*accusingly*) Where have you been, James? You've been gone ages!

JAMES Sorry, Emmsie. Grace was kind enough to show me to my room. Don't think I've had such luxury in donkeys!

GRACE I'm sure you must be more accustomed to sleeping in the middle of a volcano or a swamp. It simply wouldn't do for me I'm afraid.

ARCHIE Yes, I hear that you're a bit of a wanderer, James . . . ever got over to Oz?

JAMES Ah, breathtaking place. I was over there a couple of years back in thirty two. As luck would have it I managed to get a ticket for the first Ashes match. Suppose you've got a foot in both camps?

ARCHIE Ah, no, Ozzie through and through now. Never miss a test at the Sydney Cricket Ground.

JAMES Small world . . . we could have had a beer or three if we'd known each other then. I'm a big

fan of Bradman. Thought I might see him get a
century but it wasn't to be.

ARCHIE   Ah, yeah, I remember seeing the game . . . he
had a real stinker didn't he? But you can't have
been in Oz just for the cricket? I understand
you're a bit of a daredevil?

JAMES   No, not at all, sir . . . everything is carefully
considered. Had a bit of a moment with a tiger
shark on the Barrier Reef but luckily he was
only a fifteen footer so I managed to wrestle
him off. Close run thing though . . . I was still
weak from a touch of the dengue fever.

ARCHIE   Ah, strewth, nasty illness that one, mate . . .
we've had a heap load of cases down on the
farm. You've gotta be careful what water you're
drinking.

EMMA   (*impatient*) Come on, James, you can share all
your tales later. I'm dying to show you around.

GRACE   (*with thinly veiled innuendo*) Already done. I let
him have the full tour . . . from top to bottom.

             (GRACE *and* JAMES *exchange a discreet but
             lascivious look, which nobody else notices.*)

EMMA   But I was going to do that . . . he's my guest!

GRACE   Strictly speaking, Emma, since you now live in
London, you're both guests.

EMMA   It's still my home!

GRACE   No, darling, it's my home now . . . let's not have
any confusion about that.

EMMA   (*furious*) Uncle Archie says you're trying to
            stop his allowance . . . is that true?

GRACE   Emma, really! It's hardly polite to discuss
            delicate family matters in company. I do
            apologise, James.

ARCHIE   (*to* EMMA) You'd best pull your head in, girl.
            That's between myself and your father.

EMMA   No, I won't stay out of it! It's jolly well not
            fair. (*To* GRACE.) Until you married Daddy,
            the family never had any arguments about
            anything.

GRACE   No, of course it didn't, darling. As I understand
            it, until his death, your grandfather was the
            sole arbiter on everything . . . no argument
            entertained! If anyone stepped out of line
            they were simply dispatched to Australia or
            somewhere equally ghastly! Isn't that correct,
            Archie? Then, of course, I've heard so many
            stories about your mother.

EMMA   Don't you dare say a word about Mummy! As
            soon as she was dead you started trying to trap
            Daddy. You won't be satisfied until you've
            spent all his money . . . my money.

GRACE   Really? And that's what your father told you?
            That he only met me after your mother died?
            (*Laughing.*) Well, well. The point of it all is that
            things are rather different now . . . as you are
            surely beginning to realise.

            (WALTON *and* MORAG *enter from the hall.*)

WALTON   (*as he enters*) You'll just have to redouble your
            efforts, Mrs McKay . . . those photographs
            represent my childhood memories. (*Lightening*

and beaming broadly at them all.) So, are we all ready for the magic show? I must say I'm rather looking forward to it.

MORAG   I wouldn't be building up your hopes too high, Sir Walton. I fear the fellow is going to prove a terrible disappointment.

WALTON   Oh, come along, Mrs McKay, fair play . . . give the poor chap a chance.

GRACE   Must we really go through with this, darling? It all sounds too tiresome for words.

EMMA   Well, I think it's going to be brilliant, Daddy.

WALTON   Absolutely. Where is the chap anyway? (*Moving towards the French windows, shouting loudly.*) Pratt . . . (*Suddenly realising the relevance of his name.*) Oh, I say . . . Pratt . . . haw haw.

          (*The door to the office opens and* POTTER'S *head appears around the door.*)

POTTER   (*nervously*) Oh . . . are you ready for us?

MORAG   (*horrified*) And who gave you the authorisation to go in there? That is private office accommodation for my personal use only!

POTTER   (*stepping out into the room, apologetic*) Sorry, I didn't realise . . . wasn't my fault. Sarge said we needed a dressing room for all his bits and pieces . . . (*Pulling a face.*) you've seen what he's like.

MORAG   Well that's really not good enough, there are highly confidential papers and such like in there!

JAMES   Oh, don't be so hard on her, Mrs McKay . . .
               it's not the poor girl's fault. And, if I may say
               so, she looks an absolute delight in her fairy
               costume.

               (POTTER *is absolutely love-struck by the
               dashing and handsome* JAMES. *Throughout
               the rest of the action of the play she is shyly
               coquettish, trying to impress him whenever he
               is present.*)

POTTER   Oh, thank you. I'm supposed to be an angel
               actually.

JAMES   (*smiling disarmingly*) Oh . . . my mistake . . . a
               vision from heaven.

               (POTTER *giggles girlishly at* JAMES, *oblivious to
               everything else.*)

WALTON   Well, if your chap's ready, you'd better wheel
               him in.

               (POTTER *is oblivious to* WALTON.)

               I say . . . Miss!

POTTER   Oh, sorry, sir?

WALTON   Wheel the chap in.

POTTER   (*hoping that she's wrong*) Oh, right. You really
               want us to do this? Well don't blame me.
               (*Turning and talking through to the office.*)
               They said to wheel you in, Sarge. (*There is a
               mumbling from* PRATT *in the background.*) No, I
               don't think they meant . . . alright, Sarge.

               (POTTER *turns back to the room. Throughout
               the rest of the scene she attempts all the usual*

gestures and showmanship of a magician's
assistant but she is very self conscious which
makes her whole performance excruciatingly
embarrassing.)

He says he hasn't got any wheels . . .
(*Apologetically.*) I'm sorry, he's a bit . . .
Anyway . . . (*Clearing her throat and nervously*
reading from a written script and clearly
bemused by the various mis-spellings.) . . .
Ladies and . . . (*In an apologetic aside to*
JAMES.) . . . my hair's normally much nicer than
this but . . . (*Returning to the script.*) Ladies
and gentlemen. For your . . . (*Puzzling to make*
out the correct word.) delectation? . . . For
one night only, please be outstanding for the
Incredible Puzzled Pratt. (*With a flourish.*)
. . . Ta-da . . . (*There is an embarrassing pause*
when nothing happens.) . . . Ta-da . . . Sorry . . .
I'll just . . . (*Moving towards the office.*) Excuse
me.

(POTTER *reaches the office door just as* PRATT
appears in the entrance. He is wearing an
ill-fitting magician's tail coat and is carrying
a large top-hat. He and POTTER *have the*
following exchange in loud stage whispers.)

POTTER   We're all waiting, Sarge!

PRATT   I've mislaid the ferret!

POTTER   What?

PRATT   (*pointing at the hat*) She was just doing her last
              dress rehearsal when she skid-eggled up behind
              the filing cabinet. I can't find her.

POTTER   (*grinning*) You want to look for her under 'F'
              then, Sarge.

PRATT   What?

POTTER   'F' . . . for ferret. Joke, Sarge.

PRATT   But her name's Doris with a . . . a 'D'! Never
            mind, I'll just have to play it by eye. You see if
            you can find her . . . and put the gramophone
            record on.

            (POTTER *exits into the office and* PRATT
            flamboyantly takes centre stage.)

            Ladies and gentlemen. For your delicatessen . . .
            for one . . .

ARCHIE   Don't want to seem cranky but we've already
            been through all of that, mate!

GRACE   For heaven's sake, just get on with it before we
            completely lose the will to live.

            (*Soft background music begins to play.*)

PRATT   Very well, without further a-doodle, for my
            first trick I will astound and amaze you with
            my slate of hand. Observe that my top hat is
            currently full of absolutely nothing.

            (PRATT *theatrically waves the top hat, allowing
            the others to see that it is empty. He then places
            it on his head.*)

            Drum roll, please . . . brrrrrrrrr . . . (*Quickly
            whipping the hat from his head.*) Ta-da!

            (*The others sit and look at* PRATT *in blank
            amazement as he smiles at them in anticipation
            of applause.*)

ARCHIE   And what is it, exactly, that we're meant to be
            admiring, mate?

PRATT   Well, normally at this point there would be a
            ferret sitting on top of my head.

WALTON   Oh, good Lord, a ferret . . . on top of the chap's
            head. (*Clapping.*) That's jolly good . . . haw haw
            . . . bravo.

EMMA   But, daddy, there's nothing on his head!

ARCHIE   Or in it!

            (POTTER *enters from the office, shutting the
            door behind her.*)

POTTER   Can't see any sign of her, Sarge. Think she
            might have got behind the skirting board.

MORAG   (*alarmed*) You don't mean to say that you've
            lost the creature in my office? I can't abide to
            be in the presence of any wee animal . . . the
            mere notion makes my flesh crawl!

PRATT   You may rest assured that she is fully house
            trained and only bites on command . . . or when
            she feels like it.

MORAG   (*edging away from the office*) Sir Walton,
            I must insist that he recaptures the animal
            immediately. There's no telling what havoc it
            might cause!

            (*Throughout the rest of the scene,* MORAG
            keeps a wary eye on the office doorway.)

PRATT   All in good time, madam. My assistant has
            confided her next door. We'll allure her into the

open later with a small mortal . . . she hasn't
had any dinner so she'll be ravished.

POTTER Oh, is that why you've tried to tempt her out
with the cold tea in the saucer? Good idea.

PRATT Tea for a ferret! Are you mad?

POTTER Not as mad as you, Sarge . . . oh, sorry!

PRATT For my next trick, I shall require a small trinket
such as a diamond ring. (*Glancing around the
room and noticing* GRACE'S *ring and moving
towards her and holding out his hand.*) Madam,
if I may?

GRACE You certainly may not.

WALTON Oh, come along, my dear . . . let's get into the
Christmas spirit!

GRACE (*reluctantly taking off the ring and handing it
to* PRATT.) This is priceless . . . it's been in Sir
Walton's family for generations.

PRATT Have no fear. I will now place your ring safely
in my pocket.

(PRATT *very pointedly makes a show of
placing the ring in his pocket but then very
amateurishly pretends to cough, lifting his
hand to his mouth and clearly placing the ring
into his mouth. NB: The actor playing* PRATT
should actually leave the ring in his pocket.)

(*mumbling, because he has the ring in his
mouth*) I shall now magically produce the ring
from an inflamed balloon.

(PRATT *holds out his hand and* POTTER
*theatrically passes him a balloon from the
table. As it passes between them it is stretched
and then slaps against* PRATT'S *fingers as*
POTTER *releases her end.* PRATT *winces and
scowls at* POTTER. PRATT *makes a great
theatrical show of blowing the balloon up
before letting it accidentally blow back into his
mouth. From his startled reaction it is clear
that he has swallowed the ring. The others
watch on in shocked astonishment, realising
what has happened.*)

GRACE   You haven't!

WALTON   Oh, I say . . . he's not!

PRATT   (*flustered*) It would appear that my assistant
            has misplaced your ring, madam. However,
            she'll return it to you in due course . . .
            probably after Christmas.

POTTER   (*in horror*) Sarge . . . you're not going to . . .
            (*Giggling.*) . . . still, the Brussel sprouts will
            come in handy won't they!

GRACE   (*furious*) This is outrageous! Do something,
            Walton!

WALTON   Not sure there's anything I can do, my dear . . .
            quite extraordinary! I'm sure things will work
            out in the end.

PRATT   (*to* POTTER, *with a pained expression on his
            face*) Just pass me the cards.

            (POTTER *picks up the deck of red backed cards
            from under the scarf and goes to hand them to*
            PRATT.)

(*In a stage whisper to* POTTER.) Not those . . .
the others.

(POTTER *keeps the red cards in her hand and
picks up the deck of green backed cards from
under the scarf. She hands the green pack to
PRATT. As PRATT goes through the trick, POTTER
constantly curtsies and waves her hands in
an amateurish interpretation of a magicians
assistant.*)

(*ostentatiously fanning the pack*) Ladies and
gentlemen, I have here, in my hand, a deck
of completely unadulterous cards. (*Moving
towards* JAMES *and handing him the cards.*)

Madam, if you would please examine them and
confirm that they are completely bony fido.

(JAMES *briefly examines the cards before
handing them back to* PRATT)

JAMES   (*offering the cards back to* PRATT) Yes, they all
            seem in order.

PRATT   Oh no . . . they've been thoroughly shuttled so
            that they are totally disorderly! I thank you.

            (PRATT *moves behind* POTTER *and they try
            to discreetly, but actually quite obviously,
            exchange the cards,* PRATT *giving her the green
            backed pack and taking the red backed pack
            from her.*)

            (*playing for time*) Now, for your mesmer-
            ination . . . what I will do . . .

            (*As* PRATT *moves away from* POTTER *she
            accidentally drops the green pack behind her
            onto the floor.* PRATT *scowls at her before*

fanning out his cards as he approaches MORAG.
POTTER *takes the white scarf from the table and
makes a show of covering over the fallen cards
as though it were part of the act.*)

Please take a card . . . any card at all.

(MORAG, *who is clearly bored, attempts to take
the top card.*)

(*hurriedly*) Not that one!

(MORAG *takes another card and glances at it,
holding it close to her chest.*)

PRATT   Thank you, sir. Now, by an amazing feat of
            telephony, I will reveal to you the number
            and sweet of the card that you have elected.
            (*Holding his hand to his head as though
            exercising extreme concentration.*) Concentrate
            very hard, sir. It's coming through to me now
            . . . the card you have elected is . . . (*Letting the
            tension build.*) the seventeen of spades.

POTTER   Ta-da!

PRATT   Am I correct?

MORAG   Well of course you're not correct . . . no such
            card exists.

PRATT   (*puzzled*) Excuse me, you were clearly
            concentrating incohesively. (*Quickly turning
            the pack of cards in his hand and glancing
            at the bottom one*) Ah, I see, it was an easy
            mistake for you to make. (*Holding his hand
            to his head again.*) The card is . . . (*Pausing
            dramatically.*)

POTTER   (*feeling she should fill in the pause*) Ta-da!

(PRATT *scowls at her.*)

Sorry, Sarge.

PRATT   The card is . . . the seven of spades. Have you
          got it right this time, sir?

MORAG   Aye, so it would seem. It is the seven.

PRATT   Ta-da.

POTTER   Ta-da!

          (*They all look completely unimpressed except
          for* WALTON.)

WALTON   Oh, I say . . . well done . . . haw haw . . . very
          good.

PRATT   Thank you, Sir Walrus.

EMMA   But you used a different set of cards! They're
          red . . . the ones that James checked were
          green.

WALTON   Oh, he changed the colour as well? Oh,
          (*Clapping.*) frightfully clever.

POTTER   Ta-da!

PRATT   (*smiling innocently at* EMMA) You suspect me of
          under-arm skull-drudgery?

EMMA   Well, yes. I suppose I do.

PRATT   (*winking knowingly at the rest of his audience*)
          There is always one doubtful John Thomas.
          (A*pproaching* EMMA *and holding out the cards
          for her to pick one.*) Please, let me confound

your suspicions, young man. I will repeat the delusion. Pick a card . . . any card.

(EMMA *attempts to take the top card.*)

(*hurriedly*) Not that one.

(EMMA *picks another card and looks at it.*)

PRATT   Concentrate very hard . . . concentrate. (*Triumphantly.*) I thinks you will find that you have in your hand, the seven of spades.

POTTER Ta-da!

EMMA   Yes, I have.

PRATT   (*bowing*) I thank you.

EMMA   (*pointing at* MORAG) But she's got the seven of spades!

MORAG   (*holding her card aloft, wearily*) Ta-da.

PRATT   A coincidence I agree, but when the cards are selected randily, these statical analogies are bound to occur. For my next trick . . .

GRACE   (*standing*) I'm sure we can all find far better things to do. The man is an idiot. He's playing the buffoon.

PRATT   (*sadly*) Unfortunately, madam, I play a compendium of musical implements but have never mastered the buffoon!

ARCHIE Tell you what though, mate . . . you're the best comedy routine I've seen for years.

WALTON Oh, I say . . . buffoon . . . haw, haw . . . very witty.

MORAG (*to* PRATT, *wearily*) If I might suggest that you move straight on to your final trick, so we can all go about our business?

PRATT (*disappointed*) But what about my dancing balls and charming snake routines?

ARCHIE Ah, fair go, mate, your snake's probably far too busy chasing your ferret!

POTTER And I could get home and wash my hair, Sarge.

PRATT (*reluctantly*) Very well then, by popular bequest I shall skip straight to my climax. (*Moving to* MORAG *and stage whispering to her.*) Did you pass on my instructions as instructified?

MORAG That I did.

PRATT (*moving to* EMMA *and again stage whispering*) Are you fully convalescent with your role?

EMMA In what way?

MORAG Sergeant, if I'm not mistaken it was Lady Gates you wanted me to approach?

PRATT Indeed, I have her here now but she appears to have forgotten her briefs.

MORAG Aye, but that is Sir Walton's daughter.

PRATT Daughter? (*Bewildered, to* EMMA.) Then you're not . . . then who?

GRACE I'm afraid that would be me, Sergeant.

PRATT   (*shocked*) You?

GRACE   Yes . . . me. I'm Sir Walton's wife.

PRATT   No!

GRACE   I can assure you, yes.

PRATT   But you're far too young. (*Pointing at* EMMA.)
             She must have been a very old baby!

GRACE   I'm Sir Walton's second wife.

PRATT   What? (*To* WALTON.) Well how many wives have
             you got?

WALTON   Just the one, old chap. Couldn't cope with more
             than one at a time . . . haw haw. First one died
             I'm afraid.

PRATT   I see. (*Suddenly realising, shocked, to* GRACE.)
             But, I saw you . . . you and . . . (*Pointing at*
             JAMES.) . . . him!

JAMES   You saw what exactly?

PRATT   Well you were . . . (*Embarrassed.*) you know . . .

             (PRATT *mimes two people kissing and hugging.*
             JAMES *and* GRACE *try to disguise their guilt as
             the others look at them in shock.*)

POTTER   Sarge, I don't think you should . . .

EMMA   (*shocked*) James, what is he saying? That's
             horrid. Daddy, do something!

WALTON   Well, I'm not sure that I entirely grasp the
             chap's drift!

JAMES   (*recovering his wits and turning to* EMMA)
              Emmsie, the man is a complete half-wit. You
              surely don't believe a word. (*Approaching*
              PRATT *threateningly.*) I don't know what the
              hell you are trying to imply, Sergeant but I can
              assure you that there has been no impropriety
              on my part.

PRATT   I didn't say anything about your part!

JAMES   No . . . you have accused me of gross moral
              turpitude. I must demand that you withdraw
              your slanderous accusation, otherwise, I shall
              have to ask you to step outside and give me
              satisfaction!

              (PRATT *clearly misunderstands the meaning of
              the expression and looks at* JAMES *in horror,
              backing away from him nervously.*)

GRACE   (*laughing*) Sergeant, I'm sorry but it's just
              dawned.

PRATT   Surely not, it's past tea time.

GRACE   No, I believe I can explain your ridiculous
              mistake. Whilst you may have thought that you
              caught us in the middle of some misdeed . . . in
              flagrante delicto . . .

PRATT   I didn't say that, madam. I saw you in this room
              . . . I've never been to Spain.

GRACE   Very droll, Sergeant. (*Moving to* WALTON *with a
              slightly forced laugh.*) The man has completely
              misinterpreted what he saw, darling. You
              remember the gorgeous pearl necklace that you
              gave me when we became engaged?

WALTON   Oh, absolutely, along with your ring . . . well
            his ring for the moment.

GRACE   And it's one of my absolute favourites . . . but
            I have such terrible trouble with the clasp. It
            came loose and I simply asked James if he
            might fasten it for me. (*Laughing again.*) That's
            what this idiot saw.

WALTON   The clasp . . . oh, well . . . really, is that all?
            Puzzle solved. (*To* PRATT.) Seems like you've
            made a bit of a chump of yourself . . . haw haw.

EMMA   (*to* GRACE) But you're not wearing a necklace.

GRACE   (*reaching to her neck, slightly surprised, before
            quickly recovering and moving to confront*
            EMMA) But I was earlier. Still, I wouldn't
            necessarily expect you to notice the subtleties
            of stylish dressing, darling.

EMMA   How dare you! Daddy?

WALTON   Oh, let's not fall out about it all. I'm sure you
            didn't mean anything did you, my dear?

GRACE   Why, of course not, darling. (*Looking* EMMA
            up and down.) I simply adore Emma's outfits.
            They're so very . . . different.

            (*There is an uncomfortable silence for a few
            seconds before* MORAG *relieves the tension.*)

MORAG   So perhaps you might move on to your "climax"
            now, Sergeant. Then you can be getting away
            home to inflict your insanity on your own
            family!

PRATT   (*to* MORAG, *indignant*) I can assure you, sir
            that there is no insanity in the Pratt household.

We all have a bath every other Friday without fail. (*To* GRACE.) Have you studied your instructions?

GRACE   No, of course I haven't. I have no intention of participating in any of your ludicrous pranks. I believe I left your note in the hall somewhere.

PRATT   But you were to be randily selected to be the guinea foul.

GRACE   Well, you'll just have to randily select someone else then, won't you?

JAMES   Might I be so bold as to nominate Sir Walton to assist you? After all, he is our gracious host.

GRACE   Yes, of course, you must do it, darling . . . just because I find it tiresome . . .

PRATT   I'm afraid that I must pour hot water on that suggestion. For maximum dramatic impact I must climax with a young lady of the opposite sex.

MORAG   (*weary*) Then perhaps Miss Emma might be a suitable candidate . . . seeing as you thought it would be her in the first place!

EMMA   Me? Oh, gosh. Well, yes, I suppose it might be quite good fun! What would you like me to do?

PRATT   If you would step away this way, I will debrief you while my assistant entertains the rest of the ensemble with a joke.

         (PRATT *draws* EMMA *to one side and during the following dialogue he mimes the following routine. He indicates that she will go outside the French windows and that he will draw*

> *the curtains. He then takes a bullet from*
> *his pocket, mimes shooting a gun and then*
> *indicates that upon hearing the shot she should*
> *clench the bullet between her teeth. He then*
> *mimes that he will then open the curtains and*
> *that there will be rapturous applause.*)

POTTER (*uncertain*) Oh, well . . . I'm afraid I don't
really know any jokes . . . but my Dad says I'm
quite good at dancing so . . . here goes . . .

(POTTER *performs a short rudimentary tap*
dance routine with great enthusiasm but
extreme clumsiness, trying to impress JAMES *in*
particular. The others watch on open-mouthed
in incredulity. Starting slowly, her movements
become increasingly frantic and out of control
until she comes to an abrupt halt.)

Ta-da. (*Embarrassed.*) Wrong time of year. It's
more of a summer thing really.

ARCHIE I'll tell you a good one. There was this Pommie
Copper who reckoned he could do magic.

WALTON Oh, very good . . . and?

ARCHIE Well, that's it Walt . . . best joke I've seen in
ages. Can't wait to see his last trick . . . with
any luck he'll make himself disappear up his
own . . .

(PRATT *breaking in, having completed briefing*
EMMA.)

PRATT (*grandly*) Ladies and gentlemen. I now require
the assistance of a willy-ly-nilly-ly selected
member of the auditori-orium.

ARCHIE I reckon that'll be Emma then?

PRATT   Hold your donkey, sir . . . I have yet to make
         the selection. To ensure that my selection is
         hap-hazardous, my assistant will now make me
         unsightly with a blindfold.

         (POTTER *steps forward with the green scarf,
         curtsies and ties it around* PRATT'S *head. As she
         tightens it he winces with pain.*)

         Not so tight . . . you'll give me a brain
         haemorrhoid!

         (POTTER *loosens the blindfold a little.*)

         I have now been rendered as blind as a badger
         but to ensure that my choice is completely hap-
         hazardous, my assistant will give me a turn.

         (POTTER *makes a theatrical spin and* PRATT *lifts
         the blind temporarily to see what she is doing.*)

         Not you . . . me!

POTTER   Oh, sorry, Sarge.

         (POTTER *spins* PRATT *round several times and as
         she does so, the following exchange takes place
         in stage whispers.*)

PRATT   I can't see anything . . . you were supposed to
         use the trans-lucid one.

POTTER   Well how was I supposed to know? Shall I
         change it?

PRATT   No, they might smell a fish. Just point me in
         the right direction.

         (POTTER *stops spinning him round, pointing him
         at* EMMA.)

(*swaying with dizziness*) Please remain unmoved whilst I come amongst you to make my selection.

(PRATT *starts to walk, weaving around uncertainly as* POTTER *makes encouraging noises, trying to prompt him to move in the right direction. They all watch on in disbelief as* PRATT *eventually meanders out into the hall. A few seconds later a crash is heard. They all watch in stunned silence as, several seconds later,* PRATT *reappears with the blindfold off, blinking in the light.*)

GRACE   (*horrified*) I do trust that wasn't my Ming!

PRATT   Rest assured, madam, it was only an old vase. However, to save father time, I will employ an alternative method of selection. (*Pointing in turn at* MORAG, WALTON, GRACE *and then* EMMA.) Eeny, meeny, mini, mo . . . (*To* EMMA.) Madam, can you confirm that we have never met before?

EMMA   Well, of course we've met!

             (PRATT *shakes his head violently and puts his finger to his mouth, indicating a secret.*)

             (*heavily*) No . . . no we haven't met . . . ever.

PRATT   Then I would be obligated if you would assist me in my final trick . . . (*Dramatically.*) the catching of the bullet between the teeth. (*Turning to* POTTER, *holding out his hand.*)

POTTER   Ta-da. (*Taking a revolver from beneath the scarf, anxiously to* PRATT.) Don't you think we should open the French windows first, Sarg?

(PRATT *thrusts his hand out towards* POTTER *dismissively and she hands the revolver to him with a shrug, followed by a flourish and a courtesy.*)

PRATT   To demonstrate that there is no foul play, I will first fire an initial shot. By foul play, I don't mean that any chickens will be . . .

ARCHIE   Ah, strewth, just get on with it, mate!

PRATT   Exactly. You may wish to avert your ears.

(PRATT *takes casual aim at the French windows and fires a shot. The sound of breaking glass is heard and the curtain twitches.* PRATT *jumps at the sound of the gun. They all look at* PRATT, *open mouthed.*)

WALTON   Oh, I say . . . you've shot my window.

GRACE   (*moving to examine the curtains*) And the curtains! First the ring, then the Ming and now the curtains!

PRATT   I'm afraid it's a necessary evil, madam. You can't break an egg without making an omelette. Miss Anemone will now position herself behind the window in preparation for the (*Dramatically.*) catching of the bullet between the teeth.

(PRATT *winks at* EMMA *who begins to look very nervous.*)

EMMA   Gosh, I don't think I'm really sure about this now, actually.

PRATT   Your safety is insured, although it may be
               prudish to remove any dentures to avoid a
               choking hazard. Please?

               (*During the following conversation* POTTER
               drags a very reluctant and resistant EMMA
               *towards the French windows, opens the
               curtains and door, and shuts* EMMA *outside
               before returning to the room, closing French
               windows and curtains behind her.*)

POTTER   (*to* EMMA) It's quite safe, I checked everything
               myself. You'll be alright, honest.

JAMES   If you don't mind me saying, Sergeant, I always
               thought it was the magician who caught the
               bullet?

PRATT   Then who would fire my weapon with the
               required accuracy? To prevent further
               disfigmentation of finishings and glazing, I
               will fire the next bullet exactly through the
               previous punctuation marks.

GRACE   I shall be forwarding an account for all of the
               damages to your Chief Constable. What's he
               called?

PRATT   He's called the Chief Constable, madam.

ARCHIE   Oh, don't harass the bloke, Grace. The sooner
               he gets going the sooner we'll get shot!

GRACE   Yes, that's rather what I'm afraid of.

POTTER   All ready to go now, Sarge.

               (PRATT *mimes that she should curtsy.*)

(*curtsying and waving her arms elaborately*)
Sorry, Sarge.

PRATT (*shouting to* EMMA) Miss Enema . . . carefully
orienteer your mouth with the bullet hole in
the curtain and open wide. I will count to three
. . . on three, clench your teeth firmly together,
thus captivating the bullet before it severs your
spinal colonnade. Are you ready?

EMMA (*shouting, off*) I've been ready for ages and
ages.

ARCHIE (*laughing*) I'd clench your buttocks as well,
girl.

PRATT Drum roll please.

(POTTER *taps out an amateurish drum roll on a
piece of furniture.*)

And . . . three!

(*As he says three,* PRATT *fires a shot. There is
the sound of breaking glass and the curtain
twitches.* PRATT *smiles and bows triumphantly
while all of the others, except* WALTON, *look on
horrified.*)

WALTON Oh, bravo . . . frightfully good . . . haw haw.

JAMES Oh, my God . . . what have you done!

POTTER (*panicking*) Another pane's broken, Sarge!

PRATT Well, I can't be held responsible for the faulty
work of an incontinent glacier.

POTTER (*moving towards the curtain, anxiously*) And
there's another hole in the curtain!

PRATT   But it was already in need of darning.

POTTER   No, Sarge, that's not the point . . . you must
             have fired another live round!

             (POTTER *opens the curtains to find* EMMA
             *slumped on the ground at the other side of the
             French windows. She turns slowly to* PRATT *as*
             JAMES *pushes past her to kneel next to* EMMA.)

JAMES   Oh my, God . . . Emmsie.

POTTER   Sarge . . . I think you've killed her!

             (GRACE *screams as the others all react.*)

PRATT   (*looking bewildered for a few moments before
             trying to retrieve the situation, theatrically
             waving his hands*) Ta-da!

             (*They all look at* PRATT *in horrified amazement
             and he reacts by quickly hiding the gun behind
             his back with an embarrassed smile.*)

             (*Lights fade.*)

ACT TWO

Scene One

Five minutes later. The curtains are closed over the French window. EMMA *is sitting on a chair sobbing.* WALTON *and* JAMES *are crouched by her side, comforting her as* GRACE *and* ARCHIE *watch.* PRATT *and* POTTER *are together, a little way apart from the others.* MORAG *enters, carrying a cup and saucer.*

MORAG	Here you are, Miss Emma. A cup of strong, sweet tea will soon restore your composure.
ARCHIE	It's going to take more than a cuppa to get her right. Poor girl, she's cactus!
PRATT	Nonsense. She simply fainted into a temporary comma.
ARCHIE	What the hell were you thinking, Sergeant?
PRATT	I wasn't thinking anything, sir . . . I was simply going through my normal routine.
POTTER	Good job you're a rotten shot, Sarge . . . otherwise you might have actually hit her!
PRATT	(*indignant*) It's not my fault she didn't catch it! (*Miming catching a bullet in his mouth.*)
EMMA	There's no need to fuss. I think I'm feeling a little better now. Gosh . . . when the bullet rushed past my ear it gave me the most horrid shock!
GRACE	Walton, will you kindly throw that man out of my house this very instant. (*Fiercely, to* PRATT.) You shouldn't be allowed anywhere near a gun

... you haven't the faintest idea what you're
doing!

PRATT   (*proudly*) On the contrary, madam, my firearms
                 instructor said I was the most deadly crackpot
                 he'd ever come across.

WALTON   (*approaching* PRATT) Look, I'm frightfully
                 sorry but I think that, in the circumstances, it's
                 best that you leave, old chap. Accidents happen
                 and all that but you really do take the biscuit!

PRATT   Not for me, sir . . . Mrs Pratt will have
                 something in the oven when I get home.

JAMES   (*approaching* PRATT, *threateningly*) I've
                 travelled the world, Sergeant. I've explored
                 some very strange and frightening places . . .
                 but I can say with complete honesty that I have
                 never, ever met anyone like you.

PRATT   Oh, thank you, sir.

JAMES   If you're still within my sight in thirty seconds
                 time, I have a mind to give you a dashed good
                 thrashing, so might I suggest that you walk
                 away this instant.

PRATT   But I came by motor car.

                 (JAMES *clenches his fist threateningly.*)

WALTON   (*stepping in to intervene*) Oh, I say, we don't
                 want any fisticuffs. (*To* PRATT.) But I really
                 must insist that you leave . . . my wife is beside
                 herself.

                 (*On hearing* WALTON'S *words,* GRACE *quickly
                 lifts a hand to her head and adopts a theatrical,
                 anguished pose.*)

POTTER   (*to* WALTON) If you'll excuse us a moment, Sir Walton? Can I have a quiet word, Sarge? (*To* WALTON.) Sir?

WALTON   (*reluctant*) Two minutes then, no more . . . then I really must have you out.

(POTTER *draws* PRATT *to one side where they can speak privately, as* JAMES *returns to* EMMA'S *side.*)

POTTER   (*anxious*) I think we've got a bit of a situation, Sarge.

PRATT   Oh, it's a situation alright . . . he's not going to give us two pounds now and it's all down to your laxative behaviour. You were supposed to check the gun.

POTTER   But I did . . . there was definitely only one bullet followed by one blank. My Dad says I'm a bit scatty so I checked it three times. You know what that means?

PRATT   It means you should have checked it four times!

POTTER   (*drawing* PRATT *closer*) It means someone must have tampered with the gun.

PRATT   Ha ha . . . yes. What?

POTTER   They must have snuck along to your car, got a live round and switched it for the blank.

PRATT   And why would they do that?

POTTER   Well, because . . . (*Winking knowingly at* PRATT *who doesn't understand the meaning.*) . . . they wanted to . . . (*Continuing to wink more emphatically.*)

PRATT   (*confused*) Wink at me?

POTTER   (*exasperated*) Kill someone, Sarge! They meant
               you to fire the second live round. They knew
               everyone would just assume that it was all the
               fault of an incompetent idiot.

PRATT   And who would that be?

POTTER   Well . . . I think that's obvious, Sarge. When
               you think about it, it was a brilliant plan.

PRATT   So they wanted me . . . and you? (*Thinking hard
               for a moment.*) Exactly. I was wondering how
               long it would take you to work that one out,
               Puttle.

POTTER   So, don't you think we'd better send for
               someone, Sarge? A proper policeman . . .
               somebody who actually knows what they're
               doing.

PRATT   Somebody who knows! That is me. When I've
               solved this, think what a poke it'll give me up
               my career pole!

POTTER   I'm here as well . . . what about my career?

PRATT   Career? In case you hadn't noticed, Puttle,
               you're a woman! You don't need to be very far
               up your pole to deal with snotty kids and lost
               puppies!

POTTER   (*sulking, half to herself*) I'd heard they only
               promoted you to sergeant so they could keep
               you cooped up in the station.

PRATT   What?

POTTER   (*frowning*) Did you get permission to take that
              gun out of the armoury?

PRATT   Of course . . . as long as you filled out the
              correct paperwork, like I told you to.

POTTER   Ooh, you fibber, Sarge!

PRATT   (*turning to the others*) Your attention, please.
              It appears that there is a wolf in cheap clothing
              amongst us and I intend to root out the bottom
              of it.

WALTON   What? Good lord, what are you saying, man?

PRATT   Someone in this room thought that the
              incontinence of Constable Puddle would
              provide the perfect coverall for their plot.
              They intended to use her as their escape goat.
              When I shot upon Miss Embolism, I was under
              the apprehension that I was firing blanks.
              But unbeknownst-edly to me, someone had
              tampered with my private weapon!

GRACE   You really are being utterly ridiculous,
              Sergeant, you do realise that? Why don't you
              just go home and leave us all in peace?

PRATT   Believe me, Madam, I'm as anxious to return
              to the bosoms of my family as anybody, but it's
              my duty to implementate an investigation. I'll
              start with you and you'll soon find out whether
              I'm ridiculous or not!

              (PRATT *reaches into a pocket for his notebook
              but instead, accidentally produces a magician's
              prop such as a bunch of flowers. He hurriedly
              throws it down before successfully retrieving
              a notebook and pencil from his pocket and
              turning to* POTTER.)

You take notes as well, Puddle, you might learn
something.

POTTER   I haven't got my notebook, Sarge . . .
            (*Indicating her costume.*) there was nowhere to
            keep it!

PRATT   (*exasperated*) Well you should have tucked it
            down your . . .

POTTER   You could give me a page out of yours.

PRATT   Certainly not . . . this is mine. May Puddle
            perhaps have a piece of paper and a pencil, Sir
            Pilton, please?

WALTON   Ah, now . . . that would be Mrs McKay's
            department.

MORAG   (*wearily*) Aye, alright . . . (*Pointing at the office
            door.*) I'm still afeared of your beast mind, so
            I'll need to pop down the hallway for a wee
            moment.

PRATT   We haven't got time for that now, you'll just
            have to cross your legs like everybody else.
            Constable Piddle can help herself.

            (PRATT *gestures to* POTTER *and she exits to the
            office.*)

WALTON   Look, old chap, I hate to go on but do you
            actually have the authority to be keeping us
            hanging around like this? I mean far be it from
            me to make waves or anything like that but . . .

PRATT   Sir Wilton, my investigation is criminal, so
            if anyone is to make waves it will be me! But
            given a following wind I will sail us to the end
            of the tunnel.

JAMES   But are you actually trained for this type of
         thing, Sergeant? From what I've seen, you
         hardly seem capable of tying your own shoe
         laces.

PRATT   (*proudly*) I have a wolf cub's proficiency badge
         in knotting, sir.

ARCHIE   I suppose you'll be going off half-hitched
         instead of half-cocked then, mate!

PRATT   (*patronising, putting out his hand to indicate
         when he was a child*) Since obsolescence I
         have studied the techniques of all the great
         detectives of our time. (*Proudly.*) I have
         mouldered my technique on Hercule Puerile . . .
         have you heard of him?

JAMES   If you mean, Poirot, surely he's just one of
         Agatha Christie's!

PRATT   Quite correct, sir. One of our country's finest
         biographers.

         (POTTER *enters from the office carrying a piece
         of paper, pencil and a small piece of cloth
         matching the torn trousers that* ARCHIE *was
         wearing earlier.*)

POTTER   (*holding the piece of cloth out for* PRATT *to see.*)
         Sarge, I found this.

PRATT   Well that's not big enough to write on!

POTTER   No . . . it was on the desk by the window.
         (*Pointing to* ARCHIE.) It looks like it's off his
         trousers.

PRATT   Ah. (*To* ARCHIE, *apologetic.*) I'm so sorry, sir, it
         would appear that my ferret has consummated

your trousers. Still, we've managed to save a
small piece, so it'll be a nice little memento.
Could I have your name please, sir?

(*Throughout the following,* PRATT *and* POTTER
make occasional notes.)

ARCHIE   You already know my name, mate . . . I told you
earlier, when we met.

PRATT   Yes, but for the benefit of those who may not
know you.

ARCHIE   Well, they all know me. That's why I'm in their
house.

(*There is a slight pause as* PRATT *tries to
process his thoughts.*)

(*heavily*) Ah, let's just get it over with . . . it's
Archie.

PRATT   (*writing it down, thoughtfully*) Its-archie. That
sounds foreign, sir. Japanese at a guess?

ARCHIE   Strewth, do I look Japanese? Archie . . . Archie
Gates . . . I lived here as a boy until I emigrated
. . . (*Pointing downwards.*) down under.

PRATT   (*confused, looking at* ARCHIE *sympathetically*)
Your private medical affairs are no concern of
mine. Your reasons for re-inhibiting the house?

ARCHIE   Well, I'm just over here to visit the rellies. Walt
there's my big brother. I haven't seen him for
years.

PRATT   That seems very unusual, sir? I would make
a point of seeing my big brother regularly if I
wasn't an only child.

ARCHIE   Well, fact of the matter is that our father, in his
              wisdom, packed me off thirty years ago. I've
              got a sheep farm, near Sydney . . . New South
              Wales.

EMMA   I really don't see the point in questioning my
              Uncle. I mean, why would he want to kill me?

PRATT   My thoughts exactly. (*To* ARCHIE.) Why do you
              want to kill her?

ARCHIE   Well I don't . . . it's nonsense.

PRATT   Haha, you see. Just checking. I think that clears
              that one up. You are free to go, sir.

POTTER   I still think we need to know how a bit of his
              trousers ended up in the office, Sarge. It looks
              like he caught them on something.

PRATT   (*dismissive and condescending*) Oh, really?
              (*Spinning menacingly back to* ARCHIE.) How did
              you manage to catch your trousers, sir?

ARCHIE   Oh, that was easy enough, no worries . . . they
              can't run very fast on their own! (*Laughing,
              sharing the joke with the others, but then
              realising that* PRATT *doesn't get the joke.*) . . .
              get it . . . can't run fast on their own?

WALTON   Oh . . . can't run fast . . . frightfully clever . . .
              haw, haw.

ARCHIE   Oh, just larking with you, Sergeant. I snagged
              them on the barbed wire fence at the end of the
              paddock. I asked Mrs McKay if she'd be a sport
              and patch them for me.

MORAG   Aye, I can confirm the veracity of that
              statement, Sergeant. I took the small portion

of material through to the light so that I
could identify the best colour match. I keep a
selection of threads in there for emergencies.

PRATT   And why would you anticipate an emergency,
             Mrs Micawber?

MORAG   McKay. My name is Morag McKay . . . I've
             been Sir Walton's secretary for many a year
             . . . and his father before him. It's my job to be
             prepared for anything and everything.

POTTER   She's the one you gave the note to, Sarge.

MORAG   Aye . . . and I passed it on to Lady Gates as
             instructed, so there was no fault on my part . . .
             no fault at all.

PRATT   I beggar to differ . . . (*Pointing at* EMMA.) . . .
             you were meant to give it to her.

MORAG   But that was a case of mistaken identity,
             Sergeant . . . your mistake, I hasten to add,
             not mine. But then, I suppose you weren't to
             know that your tomfoolery would nearly end in
             tragedy . . . aye, you only averted tragedy by
             the skin of your teeth.

PRATT   My skinny teeth had nothing to do with it.
             (*Spinning to* GRACE.) So it must have been you,
             Lady Bates. You read my note and devised a
             homeopathic murder plot.

GRACE   Oh, well done . . . how astonishingly
             perceptive, Sergeant. Faced with such infallible
             logic I fear I have no option other than to
             submit myself to you. (*Melodramatic, holding
             out her hands.*) I am all yours . . . take me!

PRATT   (*embarrassed*) I don't think that would be
             appropriate, Lady Bates . . . not in present
             company.

POTTER   I think she meant take her down the police
             station, Sarge . . . but she didn't really mean it!

PRATT   Why did she say it then? (*Proudly.*) You didn't
             fool me for one moment. You planned to
             exfoliate someone and lay the blame on my
             door-stop . . . the perfect crime . . . murder by
             delusion.

POTTER   But there wasn't actually a murder, Sarge.

PRATT   Maybe not but we'll burn that bridge when we
             come to it. Lady Bates, you are under arrest.
             You do not have to take anything down but
             anything you don't say may be made up to use
             against you. Take her away, Porter.

GRACE   Sergeant . . . enough of this nonsense. I did not
             plan to kill anyone. I did not read the note. I
             left it in the hall where anyone could have read
             it. As it was addressed to me, anyone who did
             read it would believe that I was going to be
             your target. Now, to my knowledge there are
             only two persons in this room who seem to hold
             a grudge against me . . . although it comes as a
             shock that they might actually wish me dead.

PRATT   And these two parsonages are?

GRACE   Archie is convinced that I'm trying to stop him
             receiving an allowance from the family coffers.
             Darling Emma seems equally certain that I
             simply married Walton for his money. I'm sure
             it would have suited both of them if you'd shot
             me.

EMMA   That's absolutely ridiculous. I'm sorry, Daddy, I
            admit that I dislike her but I wouldn't harm her.
            Anyway, if I actually had put a real bullet in
            the gun, why would I then agree to be a target.
            I'd have to be incredibly stupid.

GRACE   Or devious.

POTTER   (*furrowing her brow, working through the
            puzzle*) I suppose, when her plan went wrong,
            if she didn't want to kill anyone else . . . she
            might agree to help and just stand clear of the
            door after we'd closed the curtains.

EMMA   Gosh, well done! That's an amazingly clever
            idea . . . but it's not what happened because I
            don't think I would ever have thought of it . . .
            I'm not really that bright.

GRACE   Well, that at least, is true, darling. Which
            brings us back to Archie.

ARCHIE   You're pretty good at firing off accusations all
            over the place, Grace. Seems like you picked
            a wrong 'un there, Walt! But let me ask you a
            question, Sergeant . . . if I really wanted her
            dead, why would I let Emma step into the firing
            line?

GRACE   Because you knew she would save herself . . .
            you were in it together. (*To* WALTON.) They were
            both ganging up on me earlier, darling. They
            were quite beastly.

WALTON   (*holding up his hands*) Enough . . . enough!
            This whole affair has gone too far. (*To* PRATT.)
            Everything is based on complete speculation.
            I mean, I know there seems to have been some
            funny business going on but . . .

PRATT   And why would you find an assault on your
             wife so funny, Sir Wilting? (*Suspicious.*) You
             said you had a previous wife who you (*Making
             quotation marks with his fingers and badly
             impersonating* WALTON.) "couldn't cope with ...
             haw haw". Did you kill her?

WALTON   No, of course I didn't . . . how could you
             possibly think that?

PRATT   Because I'm paid to think, sir. You'd be amazed
             at some of the thoughts that go through my
             head.

EMMA   Mummy died after a stupid accident in the
             garden. The coroner said she must have handled
             a poisonous monkshood.

PRATT   Indeed? And was this poisonous monk ever
             incarnated for the murder.

EMMA   No, Sergeant . . . monkshood . . . it's a plant
             . . . perhaps you would know it as wolfsbane? It
             caused multiple organ failure.

POTTER   Was she insured?

PRATT   Excuse me?

POTTER   Sorry, Sarge . . . but I'm really getting into it
             now. I think I could get quite good at this. (*To
             WALTON.*) Was she, sir?

WALTON   Well absolutely . . . yes, of course she was. All
             my family are insured. We're all worth far more
             dead than alive . . . haw haw. Oh, I say, you
             can't possibly be suggesting . . . ?

PRATT   I think we possibly are . . . (*To* POTTER.) are we,
             possibly?

POTTER   Yes, Sarge.

PRATT   In that case, Sir Wilting, if I may turn to you
               for a moment?

WALTON   Please do.

PRATT   (*turning to face* WALTON) Thank you, sir. I
               would like to delve more closely into your
               personal circumstantials? Did you late wife
               have large assets?

WALTON   Good Lord, no . . . but it wasn't important
               really. My forbears made all the money. This
               estate has been in the family for generations.
               I've been very lucky.

ARCHIE   (*bitter*) Yeah, unlike me who never got a fair
               go at all. I've been living in penury for the
               last thirty-odd years! I've had to work while
               he's been swanning about doing sweet Fanny
               Adams.

WALTON   (*indignant*) That's not entirely true, Archie. I've
               always tried to do my bit for good causes.

ARCHIE   Oh, yeah . . . that'd be right enough . . .
               the good cause being earning yourself a
               knighthood!

PRATT   Ah, so you're a Knight, Sir Wilting? Like Sir
               Gallivant on the round table. Very good.

ARCHIE   Yes, well it's all very good for him. I'll
               probably end up in a pauper's grave!

PRATT   Oh, that's highly unlikely, sir . . . I think you'll
               find that the porpoise normally buries itself at
               sea. (*Turning to* JAMES.) And what about you?

You've been curiously mutant since queering my credentials.

JAMES   Me? Oh, I've just been watching on in total awe, Sergeant. Racking my brain trying to think of anyone less suited to their profession. (*Turning to* POTTER *and smiling sympathetically.*) It must be like being led into battle by General Custer.

(POTTER *pulls a face suggesting that she agrees with him.*)

PRATT   Is there something wrong with your face, Putter?

POTTER   (*innocently*) No, Sarge!

PRATT   You want to be careful . . . if you get wind it'll stay like that!

POTTER   Could I have your name please, sir.

PRATT   George Algernon Pratt.

POTTER   No him!

JAMES   (*smiling*) Yes, of course. James Washington. Simply James would do nicely.

POTTER   Thank you, that's a very nice name. Are you married, sir?

PRATT   Yes, to Mrs Pratt . . .

POTTER   No, I meant him, Sarge.

JAMES   As it happens, no I'm not, Constable.

POTTER   (*coyly*) Mary.

PRATT   And what brings you to Sir Wilted's house?

JAMES   Just a stroke of exceptional fortune on my part.
              Emmsie invited me here for Christmas. I only
              recently returned from an expedition.

PRATT   And what were you exhibiting, sir?

JAMES   Photography. I was looking for hippopotami up
              the Jubba.

PRATT   Ah, pregnant hippopoto-mices. I'm something
              of an expert naturist myself.

JAMES   Ah . . . then you'd have been in your element.

ARCHIE   I think you're wasting you time with him, mate.

PRATT   I'll be the judge of that, sir.

ARCHIE   No . . . I'm talking to him about you!

PRATT   (*blustering*) Right, Putter, where does that leave
              us?

POTTER   (*looking at her notebook*) I don't know. Think
              I'm drawing a bit of a blank now, Sarge.

PRATT   Yes, well, it's a pity that you didn't load the
              gun with a blank like I told you!

POTTER   You loaded it, Sarge . . . I just did the checking.
              I don't suppose there's anybody else here that
              we haven't seen?

WALTON   We traditionally let the domestic staff go over
              Christmas. Cook was here earlier, preparing

this evening's cold buffet, but she left long
before you arrived.

GRACE   Speaking of which, darling, the evening is
drawing on and I think we've already wasted
quite enough time. Might I suggest that we
adjourn to the dining room? I assume you're
finished, Sergeant?

PRATT   I am never finished, madam . . . not whilst the
criminal maternity are at large.

ARCHIE   But while you're busy not solving the non-
crime of the century, I assume there's no
worries if we head through for a spot of tucker.
My stomach's starting to think my throat's been
cut.

PRATT   Very well but I must insist that no one vacate
the house until I say that you're free to depart.

MORAG   But I was hoping to be away before too long!
I'm way overdue.

PRATT   That applies to everyone, madam . . . even
expectorant mothers.

WALTON   Oh well! In that case, I suppose you'd best
set yourself a place at the dinner table, Mrs
McKay.

         (*All except* PRATT *and* POTTER *begin to exit to
         the hall.*)

GRACE   Are you sure, darling? Perhaps it might be more
appropriate for Mrs McKay to take a small
helping of food through into the office.

MORAG   Aye, well, I'm afraid that won't be possible.
              I'll not be returning to the office until the
              sergeant's recovered his vermin!

PRATT   (*indignant*) That, madam, is a valuable and
              highly trained animal.

MORAG   I rather doubt that but whatever its merits, it's
              still a loathsome wee creature. I can't abide the
              notion of it being anywhere near me!

              (MORAG *shuts the hall door as she exits last.*)

PRATT   I suppose she'd prefer a baby haggis running
              around the place. (*Looking at his notes,
              blankly.*) So, Puddle . . . what have we got?

POTTER   Potter, Sarge!

              (PRATT *waves a hand dismissively.*)

              Well, you wouldn't like it if I called you
              Sergeant Plod or something!

PRATT   (*genuinely mystified*) And why would you do
              that?

POTTER   Oh, never mind. (*Looking at her notes.*) As far
              as I can see it could have been anybody! Can't
              we just get off home . . . I've still got my mum's
              Christmas presents to wrap.

PRATT   Your mother's Christmas . . . ? And that, Pottle,
              is exactly why the female mind is not suited to
              this type of police work. You're like a fish out
              of batter.

POTTER   (*indignant*) There's nothing wrong with being a
              woman!

PRATT   (*patiently*) There's no need to get on your
               clothes horse, Pottle . . . it's not your fault you
               were born the wrong agenda. It's a well-known
               botanical fact that the female brain is smaller
               than a man's brain.

POTTER   Well, my Mum says men are useless at
               everything. (*Looking at her notes.*) I bet I can
               work this out quicker than you!

PRATT   I think not. It's all very well you taking
               cornucopias notes but you need to take
               everything they say with a pinch of snuff.
               Have the gift to read between the lines and sort
               the wheat out from the chuff. (*Looking at his
               notes.*) I mean, take that ornamental fellow.

POTTER   Who?

PRATT   Its-archie. Why would a gentleman of the
               Ornament be christened Sydney . . . and why is
               he living in South Wales?

POTTER   (*wearily*) He's an Ozzie, Sarge . . . and he lives
               near Sydney.

PRATT   (*looking at his notes more closely*) Ah yes
               . . . living in Penury . . . eating sweets with this
               Fanny Adams woman. And Sir Whittle's family.
               I have malingering doubts about them. They
               seem to be a strange bunch of coconuts . . .
               clearly from some kind of a circus background.

POTTER   Sorry, Sarge . . . I don't think I picked up on
               that.

PRATT   (*peering at his notes*) There was mention of
               four bears . . . and multiple organs. If you join
               the dots together that would suggest some kind
               of novelty animal dancing routine.

POTTER   Multiple . . . ? (*Exasperated.*) No, Sarge, that's
            what the first Lady Gates died of . . . multiple
            organ failure.

PRATT   (*impatiently*) Do try to keep up, Pottle . . . she
            was poisoned by a head monk.

            (*There is a knock on the hall door and* ARCHIE
            enters.)

ARCHIE   Sorry to barge in but I was wondering if you
            had a second?

PRATT   A second what, sir?

ARCHIE   No, I meant time for a quickie.

            (PRATT *looks at* ARCHIE *dubiously.*)

            I feel a bit of a dobber telling tales out of
            school but I didn't really want to go shooting
            my mouth off in front of the others. Fact is, I
            know one or two things that you don't.

PRATT   I very much doubt that, sir. I'm notorious
            down at the station for my prodigal width of
            knowledge.

ARCHIE   I'm sure you're notorious for all sorts of things,
            mate . . . but do you want to hear what I've got
            to say or not?

POTTER   Yes, I think we do, sir.

PRATT   Excuse me . . . I'll decide! Make a note . . .
            interview with Ozzie Its-Archie commenced at
            (*Looking at his watch.*) . . . half past something.
            (*To* ARCHIE.) I'm hoping to receive a fully
            handed time piece from Santa Claus tomorrow.

(POTTER *starts to take notes.*)

ARCHIE   Well, the thing is . . . (ARCHIE *looks cautiously
            over both shoulders to make sure that they are
            alone and* PRATT *copies him. They continue the
            routine for a few moments until finally . . .*) I'm
            not at all sure about Grace.

PRATT   Ah . . . well you would need to see a vicar for
            spiritual guidance.

ARCHIE   No, no . . . Grace . . . that's Walton's wife.
            You see I overheard her and that adventurer
            bloke conniving together in here. I could be
            wrong but I don't reckon that her story about
            the necklace holds much water. They were
            definitely up to no good.

PRATT   You mean when they were . . . (*Repeating his
            mime of two people kissing and hugging.*)

ARCHIE   I reckon so, although I didn't actually see that
            myself. Thing is, I'm between a rock and a hard
            place.

PRATT   A rock is a hard place, sir.

ARCHIE   Well, yes . . . but no . . . well yes . . . but no, I
            mean, I don't want to cause any mischief but
            from what I could gather they seem to have a
            bit of a history. I don't recall the exact words
            but I got the impression that they wanted to
            skin Walt for all his money so that they could
            go off together. I mean, it doesn't bear thinking
            about but, if you remember, they were both
            very keen for Walt to help with your bullet
            routine.

PRATT   Quite so. And?

POTTER   If Sir Walton got killed, Grace would stand to
                inherit a lot of money.

ARCHIE   Then when Emma volunteered instead of him,
                I don't suppose they would have minded her
                carcking it either. Grace hates her . . .

POTTER   . . . and it would thin down Sir Walton's heirs.

PRATT   (*disparaging*) But that's hardly an in-sur-
                mountainous problem is it? Even if he went
                completely bald he could wear a tepee.

ARCHIE   It's only my opinion mind, but if I were you I
                wouldn't trust Grace or that Washington bloke
                as far as I could throw 'em. Cunning as dunny
                rats the pair of 'em. Their stories are just a
                complete tissue.

PRATT   Bless you, sir.

ARCHIE   Thank you, just doing my bit. I'll get back
                to the tucker now but if you come through
                to check things out, (*Tapping his nose.*) I'd
                appreciate it if you didn't let on about your
                source.

PRATT   Mrs Pratt's horseradish?

ARCHIE   (*looking at* PRATT *in total disbelief, then, to*
                POTTER, *pitying*) Jeez . . . I don't envy you,
                mate. He's got about as much nous as a stunned
                mullet. Strewth!

                (ARCHIE *exits to the hall.*)

PRATT   I think that wraps things up nicely. I had doubts
                about that American chap when he started
                rambling on about pregnant rhinocer-roses.

POTTER   You mean Mr Washington? I don't think
          America comes into it, Sarg.

PRATT   Washington not America? Best leave the
          geology to me, Pothole.

POTTER   Don't you mean geography, Sarge?

PRATT   Don't change the subject. We'll take the pair of
          them down to the station to deliver the coop de
          la grass.

POTTER   But what are we going to charge them with,
          Sarge?

PRATT   Well, the pair of them are obviously complete
          cycle-paths. They may have fooled you but I
          had their numbers right up from the start.

POTTER   But don't we need some evidence? If they deny
          everything it'll just be their word against Mr
          Gates.

PRATT   Well, they may try it on with you but by the
          time I've finished with them they'll be singing
          out of my hand like a canary in two bushes.

POTTER   Are you sure, Sarge? (*Thinking hard, then, very
          excited.*) Look, I think I might have a plan.
          There could be fingerprints on the gun.

PRATT   Oh yes, very good . . . very hirsute. There'll be
          mine, yours . . . before you know it, we'll be
          arresting each other.

POTTER   But there's a chance that whoever tampered
          with the gun left their fingerprints as well.
          (*Suddenly unsure.*) I suppose they might all be
          a bit smudged by now . . .

PRATT   Exactly.

POTTER   (*suddenly excited again*) But they might not
             want to take that risk, Sarge. Suppose we
             tell them that we're leaving the crime scene
             undisturbed . . . with the gun on the table
             . . . until we can get everything fingerprinted
             tomorrow?

PRATT   Oh very good, I can see you're on the game
             . . . you're just trying to send me off on one of
             your tandems so you can go home to wrap your
             mother up.

POTTER   No, I'm not! We only pretend to leave . . . but
             what we actually do is hide.

PRATT   Hide? Like when I play Sardinians with the
             little Pratts?

POTTER   If I'm right, I reckon that the culprit will try to
             sneak in here to wipe the gun clean.

PRATT   Which we'll completely miss if we're under the
             bed or somewhere!

POTTER   But not if we hide in the right place!

PRATT   Ah . . . very good, Pothole. You got there
             eventually. I've been thatching that plan for
             some time. I shall hide in here . . . in this very
             room.

POTTER   Isn't that a bit obvious, Sarge . . . they'll see
             you straight away?

PRATT   Ordinarily they might . . . but I am a master
             of disguise. I will camouflage myself into the
             surroundings (*Adopting a still pose like a lizard
             clinging to a wall.*) like a camellia.

POTTER   Don't know how you're going to do that. What about me?

PRATT   You will patrol the exterior of the house.

POTTER   But it's freezing out there and it could take hours!

PRATT   Exactly. If Santa Claus should arrive, you must prevent him from entering and disturbing our plans.

POTTER   Santa Claus? You don't really think . . . ?

PRATT   There's no time to waste. You go and implementate my cunning ploy with the inhibitants of the house. I shall melt myself into the shadows like a nocturnip creature of the night.

POTTER   (*moving to exit to the hall with a resigned sigh*) Yes, Sarg . . . whatever you say.

      (PRATT *peers around the room to make sure that nobody is watching before stealthily creeping towards the Christmas tree as the lights fade.*)

Scene Two

Late evening. The room is in darkness except for the light from the table lamp. The card table is covered with the red and green headscarves and a bulge underneath one of them suggests that the gun is there. PRATT is kneeling near the Christmas tree, poorly disguised as a Christmas parcel. He has a Christmas paper covered cardboard box around his waist and chest and he has a ribbon tied in a decorative

*bow around his head. The door to the office is closed but
the hall door is half open, with the hallway in darkness.*

PRATT *snores quietly. A tapping is heard at the French
windows.*

POTTER   (*calling quietly from outside*) Sarge . . . Sarge,
                can you hear me?

                (POTTER *taps again but receiving no reply she
                enters the room cautiously and quietly, shutting
                the door behind her. She is still wearing her
                fairy costume but with the addition of woolly
                gloves and a scarf.*)

                (*quietly*) Sarge . . . (*Hearing* PRATT *snoring,
                louder.*) Sarge . . . what are you doing?

PRATT   (*waking himself up with a particularly large
                snort*) Haha . . . got you!

POTTER   (*accusingly*) It's me, Sarge. You were asleep.
                I'm freezing out there . . . I can't feel my toes
                or anything!

PRATT   And why do you need to feel your toes?

                (*Suddenly, a torch beam can be seen off in
                the hall, as though someone is cautiously
                approaching.*)

POTTER   (*in a loud whisper*) Hang on, Sarge, I think we
                might be in luck.

                (POTTER *quickly hides behind the curtain. A
                person, dressed in the 'ghost sheet', enters
                cautiously from the hall. The ghostly figure is
                holding a torch through the sheet so that the
                identity of the person is concealed. The ghostly*

figure moves towards the card table and reaches forward as if to try to pick up the gun.)

PRATT (*attempting to stand*) Stand and deliver in the name of the law . . . gotcha!

(*Suddenly the table lamp flickers before going out with a soft bang, throwing the stage into complete darkness apart from the beam from the torch. The ghostly figure moves quickly to the hall door and exits to the hall.* PRATT *and* POTTER *can be heard bumping around the room in the dark as they try to give chase.*)

Oh, fiddle . . . ouch . . . bother . . . come on, Pothole, get after them.

(*More banging and crashing can be heard.*)

Ha . . . Got him!

POTTER Ouch, that's me, Sarge . . . oh . . . be careful . . . hang on, you've got my . . .

(*There is further crashing and banging. Suddenly the main lights go on.* JAMES, *wearing pyjamas and a dressing gown is standing at the door with his hand on the switch.* PRATT *and* POTTER *are awkwardly entangled together on the settee.*)

JAMES Good Lord . . . is everyone alright? (*Moving toward them.*) Anything I can do to help?

POTTER Aargh, could you move your arm, Sarge, you're cutting off my circulation!

PRATT (*staggering to his feet*) I'll give you circulation, Pothole! We're perfectly fine, sir.

POTTER   You speak for yourself, Sarge . . . you nearly
            had my eye out!

JAMES   (*amused*) What on earth's been going on? Worst
            mess I've seen since I pranged the bobsleigh up
            a tree in 'thirty two.

PRATT   (*irritated*) I'll tell you what happened, sir. I
            was about to reprimand the villain when my
            assistant here assorted me!

POTTER   I didn't, Sarge . . . you were attacking me!

JAMES   I thought it must be burglars. I thought you'd
            decided to call it a night hours ago.

PRATT   Just a cunning decoy, sir, we had other ironing
            in the fire. You arrived here very quickly if I
            may say so.

JAMES   Yes, I was just heading back from the kitchen
            when I heard all hell break loose in here. I was
            feeling a little peckish. One thing I've found
            on my expeditions is that you need to listen to
            your stomach.

PRATT   I sympathise, sir. Many a night I've lain awake
            listening to Mrs Pratt's stomach. She likes a
            couple of pickled onions before she goes to bed
            but they don't seem to suit her institution.

JAMES   My commiserations. Must be dreadful for you
            . . . and her. (*Moving to exit to the hall.*) I'll
            leave you to it then.

POTTER   Just a moment, Mr Washington . . . (*Smiling
            at him.*) . . . please. (*Moving to* PRATT *and
            speaking quietly.*) Do you think we should ask
            him about the other matter . . . just in case?

PRATT   What other matter, matter?

POTTER   Mr Gates . . . he said he overheard him and
             Lady Gates. (*To* JAMES.) I'm sorry but the
             Sergeant has got a couple of little queries.

PRATT   You mean the little Pratts? (*Indignant*.) They're
             perfectly normal!

POTTER   (*giving up on* PRATT, *to* JAMES) I'm sure it's
             nothing really but Sir Walton's brother told us
             that he overheard you and Lady Gates plotting
             something. I'm sure he's wrong but . . .

JAMES   You mean he was eavesdropping on our private
             conversation?

POTTER   (*sympathetic*) I know, it's horrible isn't it! To
             be honest I don't really like him very much but
             . . . (*Looking at her notes.*) well, his exact words
             were "they wanted all Walt's money so that
             they could go off together". He seemed to think
             that you were old friends . . . but that can't be
             right can it?

JAMES   (*pensive*) Ah . . . that.

POTTER   (*disappointed*) You mean it's true?

JAMES   Well . . . sort of. What can I say? (*Playfully
             slapping the back of his hand like a naughty
             boy.*) Ha, caught in the act. It's entirely my
             fault. To tell you the truth, I've been a bit of
             a bounder, so in a way I'm not sorry that he's
             gone and let the cat out of the bag.

PRATT   Cat? That was probably my ferret.

JAMES   (*to* PRATT) Look, when you saw Grace and I
             together, it's true, we were . . . well we were

lovers once and I came here with a proposition.
I'm afraid it involved her husband, Sir Walton.

POTTER   You were going to kill him?

JAMES   Kill? Of course not . . . it was nothing like that.

POTTER   Phew, that's good.

JAMES   You see . . . some chaps I know are planning to
              have a crack at conquering Everest. Personally
              I've always believed that given a good stout
              pair of brogues and a heavyweight sports jacket
              it should be a piece of cake . . . but they insist
              on using all kinds of newfangled equipment,
              which works out to be hugely expensive.

POTTER   That sounds ever so brave . . . but I don't really
              understand the connection.

JAMES   It's quite simple. I wanted Grace to persuade
              her husband to become a benefactor and
              sponsor my place in the expedition.

POTTER   But what's so awful about that?

JAMES   But don't you see . . . I'm determined to be the
              first man to reach the summit. I'd be set up for
              life. Grace would be able to leave Sir Walton
              and I'd finally be able to keep her in some
              style. Not much of a way to repay Sir Walton, I
              know, but Grace is so miserable . . . she's bound
              to leave him eventually whatever happens. Still
              makes me feel a bit of a rotter though.

PRATT   And have you committed idolatry with her
              Grace?

JAMES   What? I absolutely worship her if that's what
              you mean. Trouble is, the whole plan's turned

out to be a complete dud from the start. She
asked Sir Walton during dinner and he refused
point-blank. Grace totally lost her temper...
said she hated him and was going to leave him.
I actually felt quite sorry for Sir Walton. He
got upset and had to leave the the room and
she went haring after him. In fact, if you don't
mind I'd rather like to cut along and see what's
happening upstairs . . . see if they're making
up.

PRATT   As you wish. Just a piece of advice though, sir,
           man to man. (*Confidentially.*) It's rather late
           and if they are making up I would leave them in
           peace to enjoy their congenital rights.

POTTER   (*hopefully*) Just before you go, I don't suppose
           you saw a ghost did you, as you were coming
           through here?

JAMES   A ghost? No, of course not . . . I don't believe
           in ghosts.

POTTER   Sorry, I just meant somebody dressed up in a
           sheet, actually.

JAMES   Ah, my mistake. Yes, I did as it happens. As
           I came through from the kitchen, I saw your
           ghost dashing up the stairs. It was quite funny
           actually . . . she seemed in rather a panic . . .
           almost as though she'd seen a ghost herself!

POTTER   She?

PRATT   Who she?

           (EMMA *enters from the hall, wearing a night
           dress and dressing gown.*)

JAMES   (*pointing at* EMMA) Well, her of course . . .
            Emmsie . . . it's her costume.

EMMA   (*startled*) Me? What have I done?

PRATT   You've been impersecuting a ghost in a sheet,
            that's what!

EMMA   What are you talking about? That's absurd, I've
            been in my room for ages. I only came down
            now because I went along to James' room and
            he wasn't there.

PRATT   And why were you going to his room?

POTTER   Don't think we want to go into that, Sarge!

EMMA   The last time I saw the sheet, it was in the
            parlour, so anybody could have taken it.

JAMES   But it was you, Emmsie . . . I saw you pulling
            the sheet off as you reached the top of the
            stairs!

EMMA   (*desperately*) James, how could you! Don't be
            so horrid, I thought we were friends.

PRATT   Oh, so you're not aware that he has erratic
            lustings for her Grace?

EMMA   He has what?

PRATT   Oh, yes, they've been having carnival
            knowledge.

EMMA   James, what is he saying? (*Accusing.*) When he
            saw you earlier, were you really . . . ?

            (JAMES *looks at her sadly.*)

But why? You were supposed to be on my side . . . not hers! (*Moving to* James, *sobbing and beating his chest with her fist.*) Oh, James, you beast . . . I hate you . . . I hate you!

(Emma *drops to her knees, having a spectacular childish tantrum, howling out loud several times and thumping the floor with her fists as the others watch.*)

POTTER   (*finally, as the last howl dies away*) I don't think you should have told her that bit, Sarge.

PRATT   This is no time for hiding the truth under bushels, Pothole. As I deducted from the start, she tried to take advantage of my magic show, to liquify her Grace, Lady Grapes.

JAMES   But why would she want to do that?

PRATT   Why? She's in high dungeon because she's just found out that Lady Grapes was having an extra maritime affair with you.

POTTER   I think the motive has to come before the event, Sarge, not after it.

PRATT   (*impatient*) Stop picking nuts, Pothole! By sneaking in here to tamper with my weapon, she has exposed herself as a ruthless, psycho-semantic murderer.

JAMES   Except, of course, nobody's dead!

PRATT   Exactly . . . a classic who didn't dunnit. Only my quick wittedness in taking inarticulate aim with my weapon prevented her from back-firing on herself. (*To* Emma.) What do you have to say to that, Miss?

EMMA   (*quietly*) It's all quite ridiculous.

JAMES   And perhaps I was mistaken? It's possible that
                it wasn't her that I saw on the stairs.

POTTER   You seemed quite certain a few moments ago.
                I know you're only trying to be kind but it
                doesn't really help. (*Kindly, to* EMMA.) I think
                you ought to tell us everything, then we can all
                go to bed.

PRATT   (*pointing at* JAMES) But not with him.

EMMA   (*starting to cry*) But I haven't done anything
                . . . honestly. Alright, I will admit that before
                the magic show I did take a sneaky look at
                your gun, Sergeant . . . but it was only out of
                curiosity.

PRATT   Once a sneak always a sneak . . . a lemming
                never changes it's spots. I put it to you that you
                tinkled with my bullets because you wanted to
                kill Lady Grapes.

EMMA   But I didn't! I mean it's hardly a secret that
                we've never got on but she's not the right
                person for Daddy at all . . . (*Pointing viciously
                at* JAMES.) as he has confirmed! But to think
                that I would try to kill her . . . that's absurd.
                (*To* PRATT.) It was sheer luck that you missed
                me with the shot . . . I've never been more
                terrified!

JAMES   I'm sorry, Emmsie but you should have told the
                Sergeant all of this earlier.

EMMA   You keep out of it. (*To* PRATT.) If I'd admitted
                to touching your weapon, you would have
                suspected me! Then, when you said about the
                fingerprints, I got frightened . . . that's why I

came down to clean it. I'm sorry, Sergeant, I'm
sure that you're probably a very nice man but,
when it comes to police work, you just seem to
guess all the time!

PRATT   So it may seem to the casual fly on the ceiling,
             but as a progeny of Hercule Puerile, I employ
             his assignation that it is not much use being a
             detective unless you are good at guessing.

POTTER   And you're really good at it, sir.

PRATT   And I'm really good at . . . (*Realising what he's
             agreeing to.*) . . . charge her, Pothole.

JAMES   Hang on, Sergeant, I don't think you should be
             too hasty. I mean, what if she's telling the truth
             . . . what then?

             (MORAG *enters from the hall.*)

MORAG   Och, so you're all hiding away in here are you?
             Since you forbad me to get away to my home,
             I've been trying to take a wee nap in one of the
             spare rooms but there's a terrible row going
             on up there between Sir Walton and his wife.
             There'll be trouble, you mark my words . . .
             terrible trouble.

JAMES   Well, why didn't you do something, Mrs
             McKay?

MORAG   It's not my place to go interfering in Sir
             Walton's personal affairs . . . I'm just his
             private secretary . . . no more than that.

             (*The sound of a shot is heard from somewhere
             distant in the house.*)

PRATT   (*startled*) What was that?

JAMES   A gun shot, Sergeant . . . if I'm not mistaken!
               Oh, my God . . . what's happened?

               (JAMES *rushes into the hall.*)

MORAG   Aye well, there you are. As I just predicted . . .
               terrible trouble!

POTTER   (*nervously*) Don't you think we'd better take a
               look as well, Sarge?

PRATT   Us? (*Frightened.*) No . . . definitely not. We've
               got all our loose ends to tie together. (*Anxiously
               looking for a safe hiding place.*) I'll take the
               prisoner (*Pointing to the office.*) through there
               out of the way. You guard the door, Pothole . . .
               if there's a phycotic homeopath on the loose it's
               your job to intersect them.

MORAG   And if I might ask, where am I to go?

PRATT   You? (*Pointing at the chair next to the table
               lamp.*) You sit down and keep quiet while I get
               on with my paperwork.

MORAG   Aye, very well, as you wish.

               (PRATT *pushes* EMMA *towards the office door
               and* POTTER *follows him.* MORAG *moves toward
               the chair and spots the table lamp cable.*)

               (*pointing*) But before you go, may I draw your
               attention over here . . . the lamp cable's been
               damaged . . . wantonly destroyed. Your wee
               beastie by the looks of it!

               (MORAG *glances anxiously around the room
               before sitting.*)

POTTER   (*moving to see the cable*) Ah . . . that's why the
              lamp went out, Sarge. Looks like Doris has had
              a real old chew at the wire.

PRATT   Oh no, not Doris! She's not died of elocution
              has she?

POTTER   (*looking around*) Can't see anything of her so
              she must be alright. (*Troubled, moving to the
              card table.*) Could I have a quick word, Sarge?

PRATT   What now? (*To* EMMA.) You stand still and keep
              quiet . . . I'll deal with you in a minute.

              (POTTER *pulls* PRATT *to one side for a private
              conversation.* MORAG *sits. Both* MORAG *and*
              EMMA *try to overhear but then feign disinterest
              as* POTTER *and* PRATT *spin to check on them.
              This can be repeated a couple of times until,
              on* PRATT's *final turn, they genuinely have lost
              interest.*)

POTTER   (*pointing to the bulge under the cloth on the
              card table, urgently*) It's just that if the gun is
              still under the scarf, it means that the shot we
              heard must have been another gun!

PRATT   Gun? Do you think I'd really be so stupid as to
              actually leave the gun there?

POTTER   Probably.

PRATT   While you were informing all the inhibitants
              about the fingerprintings, I took the precaution
              of hiding the gun. The gun-shaped gun shape
              under the scarf is just a pickled herring.

POTTER   I think you mean red herring, Sarge.

PRATT   No, it's a pickled herring. I took it off the
                buffet table.

POTTER   (*lifting the scarf*) So where did you hide the
                gun?

PRATT   (*pleased with himself*) Oh, somewhere very
                safe and secret. I went through to the hall . . .
                left the gun on the hall table while I brought the
                herring through from the dining room . . . then
                you came back and we pretended to leave.

POTTER   So the gun is?

PRATT   (*smiling*) Exactly . . . the gun is . . .

                (PRATT'S *smile gradually fades and he starts
                to look worried as he tries to remember and
                he points in different directions as he mentally
                retraces his steps.*)

                (*uncomfortably*) Well, I hope you hid it, like I
                told you to.

POTTER   Ooh . . . you're fibbing again!

                (POTTER *rushes to the hall door and peers
                cautiously through into the hall before turning
                back.*)

                It's gone, Sarg!

MORAG   It seems like you're sinking deeper and deeper
                into the mire, Sergeant. I should imagine that
                heads will roll when this comes to the attention
                of your superiors.

                (ARCHIE, *wearing pyjamas and a dressing gown,
                enters from the hall, shocked and subdued.*)

POTTER   What's happened?

ARCHIE   It's Grace . . . (*Shaking his head in disbelief.*)
            she's gone!

PRATT   Gone? Gone where? I didn't give anyone
            permission to leave. Pothole, organise a search
            party.

ARCHIE   Well you won't have far to look. I mean she's
            dead. I can't believe it . . . my own brother!

PRATT   She was your brother! Why hasn't this come out
            before?

ARCHIE   I mean she was killed by my own brother, you
            drongo! With what looked like the very same
            gun you were fooling around with earlier.

MORAG   (*accusingly at* PRATT) The same gun was it? But
            I canna believe that Sir Walton would ever do
            such a thing, you must be mistaken!

ARCHIE   I could hear them having a row in her room. All
            hell let loose . . . Walt was as angry as a frog in
            a sock. Then there was a shot. I dashed out and
            there he was, standing in the doorway with the
            gun in his hand. I managed to grab it off him,
            just as (*Pointing at* EMMA.) your bloke arrived.

EMMA   He's nothing to do with me! Where's Daddy
            now?

            (JAMES *enters, holding* WALTON *by the arm.*
            WALTON *is wearing pyjamas and a dressing
            gown.*)

JAMES   (*visibly shocked and upset*) He's here. (*Roughly
            pushing* WALTON *into the room.*) Get in there.

WALTON (*distressed*) But Grace . . . we must get her
      some help!

ARCHIE She's beyond help, Walt . . . she's got a hole in
      her head the size of a footy ball!

WALTON But I was only talking to her a few minutes
      ago.

JAMES Talking? You were having a hell of a row,
      that's what you were doing! All because Grace
      saw you for what you really are . . . a useless,
      puffed up, pathetic piece of . . .

EMMA (*running to* WALTON'S *side*) I don't care what
      you've done, Daddy . . . she's just been using
      you.

PRATT (*indignant, to* EMMA) I told you to stand over
      there. Reprehend him, Pothole.

      (POTTER *moves to* WALTON. *Not knowing what to
      do she finally holds his hand.* WALTON *looks at
      her in surprise.*)

POTTER (*apologetic*) I'm sorry, I've never done this
      before.

JAMES I'll never forgive myself, Sergeant . . . I should
      never have left them together. (*To* WALTON.) I'll
      make damn sure you pay for this!

PRATT Ah . . . now, now, Mr Washingup . . . you
      must leave all of this in the hands of we
      professionals. I'm afraid we have to go through
      the fertility of a fair trial before we're allowed
      to hang him.

MORAG Well in my humble opinion you've not been
      very professional so far, Sergeant. If you hadn't

turned up with that gun this afternoon none of
this would have happened . . . none of it at all.

PRATT   But that's just where you're wrong, Mrs Mucky.
It was clear to me from the start that this whole
household was (*Nodding knowingly at* ARCHIE.)
a seething box of frogs in socks! Charge him,
Pothole . . . (*Pointing at* EMMA.) and her as well,
just to be on the safe side.

WALTON   But I haven't done anything! The only reason
we were arguing earlier . . . (*Pointing at* JAMES
accusingly.) was because of him . . . he's a . . .
a dashed bounder! It was all giving me a jolly
rotten headache so I went back to my room.
When I heard the shot I trotted out and found
the gun lying in her doorway. She was just in a
heap on the floor.

POTTER   So what are you saying, sir? That she shot
herself?

JAMES   Ah, poppycock, Grace would never have done
that!

POTTER   (*to* ARCHIE) Well that just leaves you then, sir.
We've only got your word for what you say you
saw.

PRATT   Nonsense. I can see what happened as clear as
night. Lady Grapes got up Sir Watford's goat
when she told him all about the size of Mr
Washingup's huge equipment.

(POTTER *giggles uncontrollably.*)

What?

POTTER   (*trying to stifle her laughter*) Sorry, Sarge,
              I know this is serious but that was a bit of a
              double entendre . . . about Mr Washington's . . .

PRATT   No it wasn't . . . just pull yourself together. If
              you want a proper double entendre just you wait
              and I'll give you one! Handcuff Sir Wilting
              while I go upstairs and examine the copse.

POTTER   (*pointing at her costume*) I haven't got any
              handcuffs, Sarge.

PRATT   Tie him up then! (*Looking around and pointing
              to the card table.*) Mrs Monkey, pass her the
              green scarf will you?

MORAG   Oh . . . aye, the scarf.

              (MORAG *looks hesitant for a moment before
              picking up the red scarf and moving towards*
              POTTER.)

PRATT   (*patronising*) No, I said the green scarf, dear!
              That red one's Mrs Pratt's Sunday best.

MORAG   (*hesitant*) Ah, it's the green you're wanting. I'm
              sorry, Sergeant . . . my mistake . . . I must have
              misheard.

              (MORAG *moves back to the card table to swap
              scarves.*)

POTTER   (*frowning*) Hang on a minute, Sarge.

              (POTTER *move towards the card table, picks up
              the green scarf and takes the red scarf from*
              MORAG. *She puts the scarves behind her back
              and mixes them up.*)

PRATT   What are you doing? This is no time for more
             tricks.

POTTER   (*holding the scarves up in front of* MORAG, *one
             in each hand.*) Which one is the green one?

             (MORAG *hesitates.*)

             You can't tell can you? You heard him alright
             but you're colour blind!

MORAG   Aye well, maybe so but a visual impairment is
             hardly against the law!

PRATT   Exactly. (*Pointing to his right eye.*) I myself am
             inflicted by a slight stigmata in my left eye.

POTTER   But don't you see, Sarge?

PRATT   Not as well as I would with forty forty vision
             but I can still drive.

JAMES   Well I'll be . . . you're right. She claimed that
             she'd taken the cloth from Archie's trousers
             through there so she could choose the best
             colour match!

POTTER   Green trousers. (*To* MORAG.) It would have been
             impossible for you to match the colour. Why
             were you lying? Were you trying to cover up
             for him? (*Pointing to* ARCHIE.) When we first
             met, you said you'd just been for a walk (*With
             sudden realisation.*) but if that's true, how did
             you overhear Mr Washington talking to Lady
             Gates in here? You certainly weren't outside,
             we'd have seen you.

JAMES   Well he wasn't in the hall when we went out.
             He must have been through there, in the office.

WALTON   Oh, no . . . no, he wouldn't have been in there
                . . . that's Mrs McKay's domain.

POTTER   (*to* ARCHIE) When I found the fragment of cloth
                it was by the window. That's where you tore it
                . . . on the window catch. Why did you need to
                climb out?

JAMES   If you ask me there's some funny business
                going on between them, Sergeant . . . I had a
                feeling earlier that there was something not
                quite right about him. (*To* ARCHIE.) You don't
                get dengue fever from drinking bad water . . .
                it's from mosquitos!

ARCHIE   (*aggresive*) Oh, and you know everything do
                you, mate? I don't know what all this is about,
                Sergeant. I tell you the honest truth about what
                I saw up there and this bloke wants to castigate
                me.

PRATT   Oh, I don't think he'd go that far, sir.

JAMES   (*becoming increasingly annoyed, to* ARCHIE)
                And you're certainly not the true Ozzie cricket
                fan that you wanted me to believe. No . . . no,
                in Sydney, Bradman didn't have the stinker of
                a game you claimed to see . . . he wasn't even
                playing!

PRATT   (*to* ARCHIE) Is that true? Did you really see this
                Sydney Bradman or is he just an imaginary
                friend . . . like I sometimes imagine I have
                friends?

POTTER   Hang on, Sarge. I think I've got it now.
                (*Proudly, pointing to the office.*) Remember the
                cold tea I found in the saucer? I thought you'd
                put it down for Doris but it must have been
                there from earlier. He tipped it in there so that

he could use the cup to listen through the door
. . . I used to do that when I was a kid!

ARCHIE   (*losing his temper*) Ah, well you're a very clever
              madam aren't you?

POTTER   I don't like this at all, Sarge. I think we should
              take them all down to the station.

ARCHIE   (*glaring at* POTTER) And you think I'm going
              anywhere with you! You don't want to take any
              notice of this one, Sergeant, she's way out of her
              depth. Anyway, I've got to be out of here first
              thing in the morning . . . I've got a train to catch.

POTTER   (*triumphantly*) Ha . . . no you have not! There are
              no trains on Christmas Day . . . so there!

              (*Sticking out her tongue at* ARCHIE.)

ARCHIE   (*moving to give himself space and pulling the
              gun from his pocket and pointing it threateningly
              and then speaking in an English voice*) Yes, well
              like I said . . . it turns out you're too clever for
              your own good.

              (*They all pull back from* ARCHIE *a little with the
              exception of* JAMES *who starts to move towards
              him.*)

JAMES   You murdering . . .

ARCHIE   (*aiming at* JAMES) You keep back . . . unless you
              want to be next.

              (JAMES *stops in his tracks.*)

PRATT   (*to* POTTER) Now look what you've done! I was
              just about to pounce and disable him with a blow
              to the solar plectrum.

MORAG   Aye, well I hate to say it but I've had my
             reservations, Sir Walton. He's a fraud . . . aye,
             nothing but a fraud! I could see it from the
             start.

ARCHIE   (*to* MORAG) And don't you think I'm going to
             carry the can for this on my own. You got me
             into this mess . . . you can damn well think of a
             way out!

WALTON   Mrs McKay? You and her? Oh, I say . . . I don't
             believe it!

MORAG   (*angrily, to* ARCHIE) And just why did you
             want to go opening your big mouth like that?
             (*Moving to* ARCHIE'S *side.*) It's exceedingly good
             money I've been paying you to play your part.

EMMA   What are you doing, Mrs McKay? I thought we
             were your friends?

MORAG   Friends? Since when have the bone idle Gates
             family been friends of any honest hard working
             folk? Over thirty years I've been working my
             fingers to the bone for a pittance . . . a mere
             pittance!

WALTON   But I thought we were a team, Mrs McKay. And
             why are you doing this, Archie? If it's simply
             money, I'm sure we could have come to some
             kind of accommodation.

MORAG   Archie? (*Smirking.*) I hate to be the bearer of
             bad news, Sir Walton, but dear Archie's been
             dead for these past twenty five years. Being the
             black sheep of the family, I suppose it was quite
             appropriate that he drowned in the sheep dip.

WALTON   What? No! But the payments! (*To the others.*)
             When father dispatched Archie to Australia, he

set up a fund to provide him with a quarterly income . . . he didn't trust him to handle a large lump sum because that's why Archie ended up in trouble in the first place . . . huge gambling debts.

MORAG   And being the lackadaisical, uncaring so and so's your family are, all of the financial dealings and correspondence were conveniently passed through me . . . in and out . . . I handled it all . . . aye, everything.

WALTON   Good Lord!

MORAG   So, all these years I've been building up a nice little nest egg . . . squirrelling money away to help me get by.

PRATT   But now all your squirrels have come home to roost at once.

MORAG   Aye well, I suppose it couldn't last for ever. (*To* WALTON.) It was all going very smoothly until your first wife foolishly persuaded you to have a reconciliation. As you can imagine, I wasn't too keen on you making the journey to Australia . . . it would have rather given the game away.

EMMA   Lucky for you that poor Mummy died.

MORAG   (*smirking*) Aye . . . such an unfortunate accident. When you decided you'd take her place on the trip I had to immobilise your father with the cricket bat. I'm sorry, Sir Walton but I must admit that I did derive enormous pleasure from the exercise. I had to make sure your family reunion took place over here. I have a cousin in prison and he was able to recommend Reginald here.

PRATT   Ah but you didn't count on me turning up and
             upsetting the apple tart.

MORAG   You were a godsend, Sergeant. Grace was
             getting very tiresome in her insistence that
             Archie's payments should be stopped and Sir
             Walton is easily led. I read your note and saw a
             chance for you to shoot her for me. It was I who
             meddled with the gun.

EMMA   But he nearly ended up killing me instead!

MORAG   I saw no need to intervene . . . it would have
             been my gift to the rest of humanity. (*To*
             PRATT.) You bungled the shooting but then your
             carelessness with the gun presented another
             chance. We all heard Grace and Sir Walton
             arguing. With her dead and him framed for
             murder, it would have been easy to manipulate
             Emma . . . she's hardly the brightest, even
             compared with the rest of the family. It's a pity
             your assistant has rather more brains.

POTTER   Oh, thank you! But I don't understand why he
             climbed out of the window earlier . . . that's
             what gave it all away in the end.

MORAG   Sir Walton came in here and trapped Reginald
             in the office while I was briefing him. By the
             way, Sir Walton, I'm afraid I had to burn all of
             your old photographs. Reginald has an uncanny
             resemblance to Archie but it seemed prudent to
             eliminate any risk of comparison.

POTTER   So what are you going to do now?

MORAG   Aye, well, that's a very good question. Reginald,
             pass me the gun, if you please, I have a wee job
             for you.

(ARCHIE *carefully passes the gun to* MORAG
*who immediately moves away from him and
stands by the fireplace with her back to it. She
then points the gun at* ARCHIE *whilst carefully
keeping her eyes on the others.*)

Thank you, I'm most obliged. Now would you
care to join the others over there.

ARCHIE   Me! What are you up to?

MORAG   I'm afraid you're of no further use to me
            and I'm not inclined to pay you for your
            incompetence. You've been a terrible
            disappointment with your catalogue of mistakes
            and your ridiculous Australian accent. If you'd
            all lie down on the floor, please.

PRATT   If anything happens to me you'll have Mrs
            Pratt to answer to and she's a very frightening
            woman after dark!

MORAG   Well I'm afraid I'll just have to risk that.

            (*An insistent scratching noise can be heard
            from the fireplace.*)

JAMES   (*dramatically*) Just hold on a moment . . . I can
            hear something. What's that noise?

MORAG   Noise? Don't be wasting your time with such
            nonsense . . . you'll have to try harder than
            that, Mr Washington!

POTTER   No, he's right. I can hear it as well.
            (*Dramatically.*) It's behind you.

MORAG   Och, no it isn't. Just because it's Christmas,
            don't go thinking I'll be joining in with your
            pantomime japes.

PRATT   But it is . . . it's coming from the chimney.
               (*Excitedly.*) It must be Santa Claus . . . he's
               coming to save us from being slayed to death.

POTTER   (*pointing behind* MORAG) No it's not . . . look,
               it's Doris!

                    ENDING NUMBER ONE

               (MORAG *screams and spins round in alarm,
               panicking. In the confusion,* JAMES *and* POTTER
               leap forward, pouncing on MORAG *and quickly
               restraining her as* ARCHIE *bolts towards the
               French windows.*)

WALTON   Oh, I say . . . jolly well done!

MORAG   (*still screaming, terrified*) Keep that beast
               away from me!

POTTER   (*seeing* ARCHIE *exit through the French
               windows*) Sarge, be quick!

PRATT   (*uncomprehending*) What?

JAMES   Well, don't just stand there you fool . . . give
               chase!

PRATT   Ah, right. Exactly.

               (PRATT *looks around in confusion before
               running out into the hall, shouting, as the
               others watch on in amazement.*)

               Doris . . . here girl . . . come to Daddy Ferret . . .
               Doris . . . Doris.

(*The others slowly turn to look at* POTTER *with questioning expressions. Sensing their eyes on her she shrugs helplessly.*)

ALL   (*in unison except for* MORAG *who remains silent*) Pratt!

ALTERNATIVE FARCICAL ENDING

(DORIS *can be seen in the fireplace.* MORAG *screams and spins round in alarm, panicking. In the confusion,* JAMES *and* POTTER *leap forward, pouncing on* MORAG *and quickly restraining her. As they struggle, a shot is fired into the air from her gun. As this is happening,* ARCHIE *rushes out into the hall, only to return seconds later clutching at* DORIS *who has him by the throat.* ARCHIE *falls onto the settee still trying to wrestle* DORIS *away.* PRATT, *meanwhile, wanders around in confusion or, if he is still wearing the box disguise, trips onto the floor and is unable to stand again.* SANTA CLAUS *suddenly appears through the French windows, waving to everyone as the lights fade.*)

PROPERTY LIST

ACT ONE

Scene One

Set: Fireplace in which a fire is lit. Christmas tree, decorated with tinsel and baubles. Wrapped presents (including PRATT's disguise box) under tree. Sideboard with telephone, decanters and glasses. Settee with low occasional table in front with ash tray. Small table. Four Chairs. Low table, upon which is a table lamp. Documents and files are haphazardly strewn around the room.

Personal: Collection tin, handkerchief, instruction note, Santa beard & hat (PRATT).

Scene Two

Strike: Used glasses, remains of smashed bauble from table, Santa beard and hat.

Set: All doors and curtains closed. Insert broken pane in French windows. On table, centre left, red and green packs of cards covered by green scarf, gun covered by red scarf, white scarf, balloons.

Insert second broken window pane after EMMA exits through French windows and curtains are re-closed (page 60).

Offstage: White ghost sheet (EMMA).

Personal: Book (ARCHIE).

Ring on finger (GRACE).

Top hat (PRATT).

Script (POTTER).

ACT TWO

Scene One

Strike: Playing cards, balloons, book, white sheet.

Set: Red and green scarves and gun on table, centre left.

Offstage: Trouser fabric, paper and pencil (POTTER).

Personal: Cup and saucer (MORAG).

Magician's prop, notebook and pencil (PRATT).

Scene Two

Strike: Gun

Set: Small object under red scarf on table, centre left

Personal: Gun (ARCHIE)

LIGHTING PLOT

ACT ONE, Scene One: Dimly lit room. Only apparent source of light from outside French windows and fire.

MORAG: "Aye, whatever you say, Sir WALTON . . . (*Moving to the table lamp and switching it on.*)

Page two: Lamp lights and illumination increases, predominantly stage left.

MORAG (*moving to the main light switch and turning it on*)

Page two: Overall lighting rises to maximum.

ACT ONE, Scene Two: Fire and table lamp lit. Full lighting. Dark outside French windows.

ACT TWO, Scene One: Fire and table lamp lit. Full lighting. Dark outside French windows.

ACT TWO, Scene Two: Dimly lit room. Fire dark. Only apparent source of light from table lamp.

PRATT:"Stand and deliver in the name of the law . . . gotcha!".

Page 89: *Table lamp flickers then goes out leaving stage in darkness.*

POTTER: "Ouch, that's me, Sarge . . . oh . . . be careful . . . hang on, you've got my . . . "

Page 89: *After several seconds, lighting on to maximum.*

EFFECTS PLOT

Cue one: GRACE:"For heaven's sake, just get on with it before we completely lose the will to live."

Page 43: *Soft background music begins to play.*

Cue two: PRATT (*Blindfolded, exits into the hall.*)

Page 58: *Loud crash of a breaking vase, offstage right.*

Cue three: PRATT: "Exactly. You may wish to avert your ears" (PRATT *takes casual aim at the French windows and fires a shot*).

Page 59: *Sound of breaking glass and the curtain twitches.*

Cue four: Pratt: Drum roll please." (Potter *taps out an amateurish drum roll on a piece of furniture.*) "And . . . three!"

Page 61: *Sound of breaking glass and the curtain twitches.*

Cue five: Pratt: "Stand and deliver in the name of the law . . . gotcha!" (*Suddenly the table lamp flickers before going out with a soft bang.*)

Page 89: *Soft bang offstage left as lights go out.*

Cue six: Morag: "It's not my place to go interfering in Sir Walton's personal affairs . . . I'm just his private secretary . . . no more than that."

Page 97: *Gun shot, offstage right.*

Cue seven: Morag: "Well I'm afraid I'll just have to risk that."

Page 111: *Insistent scratching noise behind fire, stage right.*

GEORGE ALGERNON PRATT – A brief biography

Much of Pratt's early childhood is shrouded in mystery. Born to loving parents, it is unclear why they made several attempts to foster him into other people's care, only for him to be returned within a short period of time. What is known, however, is that in his teenage years he developed a fascination with flying. Sadly, events conspired against him pursuing his career of choice. After several flying lessons and the loss of a number of aircraft he was advised to seek alternative employment. This was undoubtedly a bitter blow. As he himself remarked in later years, "My failure in the aviary industry left me feeling as though I was trapped in a cage".

Shrugging off this early disappointment, Pratt's legendary resilience came to the fore and his love of animals led him to train as a veterinary surgeon. Regrettably, this vocation also had to be abandoned following a serious incident with a goat. It was at this momentous point in his life that he decided to dedicate himself to public service as a police officer and the rest, as the saying goes, is history.

Unfortunately, much of this history has been lost with the passage of time. Being rapidly transferred through a number of different forces, his early work is unrecorded. Rumours of the suicide of some of his senior officers are largely unsubstantiated but there appears to be some truth in the tale of a cycling accident. The resulting destruction of a police box and related head injury may, in part, account for some of his later social and linguistic difficulties.

It is known that Pratt's promotion to Sergeant was the result of an administrative error but it was from this point onwards that he finally made his mark in the force. Full details of many of his cases were lost in the fire when he was preparing to write his autobiography shortly before his death at the age of ninety three. We are, therefore, indebted to his biographer, Peter Gordon, who has meticulously researched and presented some of his better known cases in dramatic works on the stage.

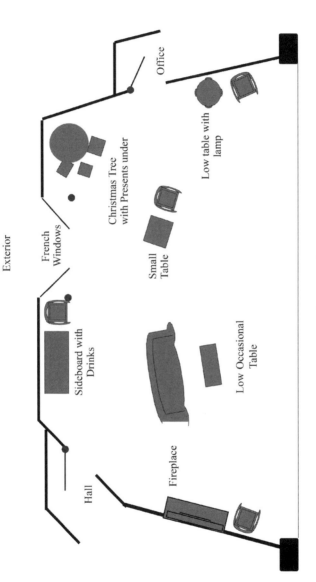

Sleighed to Death - Set

Office

Low table with
lamp

Christmas Tree
with Presents under

French
Windows

Exterior

Small
Table

Sideboard with
Drinks

Low Occasional
Table

Fireplace

Hall